James Joy
and t
Craft of Ficti

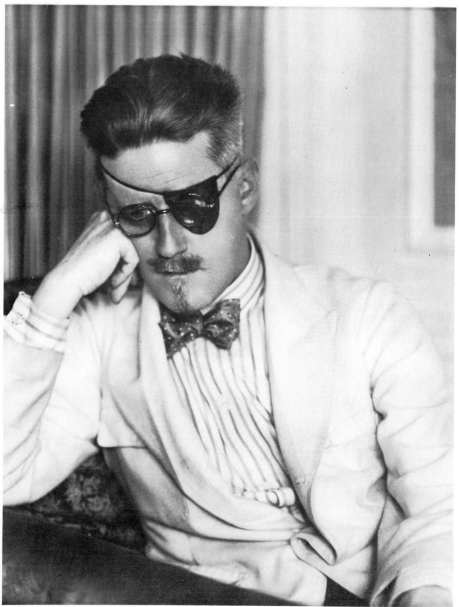

James Joyce

James Joyce
and the
Craft of Fiction

An Interpretation of *Dubliners*

Epifanio San Juan, Jr.

Rutherford • Madison • Teaneck
Fairleigh Dickinson University Press

Other books by Epifanio San Juan, Jr.:

The Art of Oscar Wilde
A Casebook of T. S. Eliot's "Gerontion"
Critics on Ezra Pound
The Radical Tradition in Philippine Literature

© 1972 by Associated University Presses, Inc.
Library of Congress Catalogue Card Number: 71–180647

149440

Associated University Presses, Inc.
Cranbury, New Jersey 08512

ISBN: 0–8386–1078–1
Printed in the United States of America

For
KARIN
and
ERIC

CONTENTS

PREFACE

This book aims to present what, to my knowledge, has so far been lacking in the corpus of Joycean criticism: a formal analysis of each story in *Dubliners* conceived as a distinct integral whole, with parts arranged in a unique sequence, producing an emotional and intellectual effect commensurate to the interaction of the parts in the whole. My job is primarily the explication of pattern—how the elements of the pattern combine, the nature of the combination, and its capacity for evoking response. My single controlling assumption is that the type of fiction which is not allegorical or didactic falls under the category of mimetic art. The aesthetic rationale of this imitation manifests itself in the power or principle that energizes the parts of the work and unifies it in a dynamic configuration producing the effects contemplated by the artist.

In the process of explication, I have tried to allow the movement of the story itself to guide the order of the interpretive discourse. Consequently I have not insisted on the strict application of categories, or on the finer theoretical distinctions between plot and episode, and so forth, for all these are subordinate to the primary objective of educidating the action of each story. If there is one criterion of evaluation I have adhered to, it is the primacy of plot as the means of embodying the action of

9

the narrative. While not discounting the symbolic and metaphoric "ambiguities" of each story or of *Dubliners* as a whole, I have chosen the altogether different task of defining the action of each story by analysis of the plot. This task assumes the need to distinguish the emotional effects of each story by determining their causes in the formal elements, the qualities of the parts, and their synthesis. For in describing the unifying action of a story, one also describes the causes of our reading reactions, on both emotional and intellectual levels.

Since I consider the action imitated by the plot as decisive in understanding the distinctive whole of a fictional work, and thus restrict myself to the problem of elucidating this larger structure, the reader should not expect a discourse on myth, symbol, religious or theological overtones, sources, allusions, cultural background, and the like, all of which can sufficiently be found in the numerous articles on Joyce listed in the annual bibliographies. Such pieces of information as are needed and thought relevant to reinforce the premises of my argument will be used accordingly. I am therefore indebted to all the scholars and commentators who, by their collective endeavor, have cast light on the individual stories from different angles and perspectives.

The insights and judgments of Joycean scholars have either prompted me into clarifying their assumptions about *Dubliners* in the framework of each story's action, or challenged me into searching for other ways of elucidating narrative form. If the method used here aims to contribute anything to our appreciation of *Dubliners,* it is that of articulating the experience of form as the groundwork for any further interpretation of meaning. For the "ideal reader" whom Joyce conceives as blessed with insomnia, any attempt at elucidating Joyce's craft of fiction in *Dubliners* is its own reward.

The task of interpretation, I believe, is oriented to the

end of enlarging and clarifying the reader's perceptions—
his whole emotional and intellectual response to the literary work. If I have pointed out with any accuracy the
informing principle of each story, the reasons why the
work affects us in the manner it does, then the complete
formulation of symbolic meaning and other implications
of universal significance will be the reader's privilege to
accomplish. Given the acknowledged greatness of *Dubliners,* I suppose no further argument is needed to justify
the choice of the work as a subject for critical reflection.
The "meanings" of Joyce's stories are virtually inexhaustible and constitute a permanent possibility of experience for all.

ACKNOWLEDGMENTS

The writing of this book dates back to 1967 when I was awarded a small grant by the University of the Philippines Research Office. The research, final writing, and revisions of the work were immensely facilitated by faculty research grants from the Research Foundation of the University of Connecticut, Storrs, for which I am thankful.

I also wish to acknowledge here my gratitude to The Viking Press, Inc., for permission to reprint excerpts from *Dubliners* by James Joyce. Originally published by B. W. Huebsch, Inc. in 1916. Copyright © 1967 by the Estate of James Joyce. All rights reserved. Reprinted by permission of The Viking Press, Inc. I also thank the following journals for permission to use materials which first appeared in their pages: *University Review, Eire-Ireland, Archiv für das Studium der Neueren Sprachen und Literaturen, Research Studies, Die Neueren Sprachen,* and *Revue des Langues Vivantes.*

To my wife Delia Aguilar-San Juan, without whose generous help and warm encouragement this book would never have been completed, I owe much more than can be expressed here.

INTRODUCTION

Readers of *Dubliners* who have been strongly affected and deeply moved by the individual stories would certainly acquire fuller insight and understanding of the art of fiction if they asked themselves the causes of their own emotional and intellectual responses to a story they are reading. The criticism of fiction is in a fundamental sense an inquiry into the dynamics of our reading experience, an endeavor to discriminate among the possible ways of responding intelligently and sensitively to a literary work. A modern tendency to explain our experience as reactions to symbols, metaphors, and imagery seems, however, to reduce the experience to a matter of assembling formulae in which an image represents an idea, and a character or event stands for a metaphysical norm or an archetypal myth. To elucidate the form of a story in an allegorizing manner is to limit drastically the experience of fiction to a grasp of abstract ideas open to sophistic refutation.

It is commonplace to note that Joyce radically departed from the formula-oriented modes and devices of the plotted story aimed at melodramatic effects. Instead, he chose the form of the "plotless" story in the tradition of Flaubert and Henry James. Scholars have pointed out the clusters of images, metaphors, and symbols—including constellations of archetypes—around which the other elements

15

of the story gravitate.[1] Emphasis on verbal texture, on the other hand, has led to the concentration on "tonal suggestiveness," "emotional coloring," and timbre of vibrations, as though each story as a unified whole, possessing Joyce's three qualities of beauty—integrity, consonance, and radiance—could be apprehended by dealing with the parts. Modern criticism of fiction has assumed the synecdochic approach of working from the part conceived as a microcosm to be a valid and accurate way of grasping the shaping principle of the whole work.

If we examine Joyce's own pronouncements on the imaginative process and extrapolate from such data his own theory of narrative form, we shall find that the allegorizing mode, usually characterized by critics as Joyce's typical method of executing his fiction, is quite contradictory to the artist's own conception of his art. The best critical procedure for testing the validity of the prevailing fashion in interpreting *Dubliners* is, of course, to analyze the stories themselves and discover what kind of artistic wholes they are. But it might be a profitable orientation for the reader of the following explications to review Joyce's aesthetic theorizings to see whether they might lend substance to the hypotheses and logical presuppositions of the commentaries in this book and credence to the conclusions arrived at. In analyzing the causes of our complex reading experience, however, the writer's own ideas of what he is doing can function only as point of departure, never as the *a priori* standard of correct evaluation, for the work itself might even belie the artist's interpretation. At best, the artist's testimony can reinforce the relevance of certain observations and rule out farfetched analogies.

---

1. See such representative studies as: Brewster Ghiselin, "The Unity of Joyce's *Dubliners*," *Accent* 16 (Spring, 1956) : 75–88, (Summer, 1956) : 196–213; Marvin Magalaner, *Time of Apprenticeship: The Fiction of Young James Joyce* (New York: Abelard-Schuman, 1959) ; Gerhard Friedrich, "The Perspective of Joyce's *Dubliners*," *College English* 26 (1965) : 421–26.

The value of the interpretations offered here rests entirely on how well they can explain the tremendous power and interest of the stories themselves.

In a letter to a friend in 1904, Joyce confessed that his purpose in writing the stories in *Dubliners* was to "betray the soul of that hemiplegia or paralysis which many consider a city."[2] On the basis of this general intention, each of the stories may be construed as a means of demonstrating a thesis—the underlying theme or argument of the work. But if we consider each story as an integral whole, with a form realizing an aesthetic purpose implicit in its organizing principle, what we shall be confronted with is a diversity of means adjusted to a corresponding diversity of ends.

The theme of paralysis serves as a unifying concern which embodies the value of the material out of which the stories were shaped, but it never embodies the principle of organization as such.[3] This uniformity of concern can hardly be endorsed as a central, guiding objective without being vitiated by the author's own reservations. Combining passionate sympathy and critical detachment, Joyce on the evidence of his letters persuades us to take a balanced if not positive view approximating the artist's in formulating the ultimate emotional effects of each story. Writing to his brother Stanislaus about the unsatisfactory milieu rendered in "The Dead," he criticizes his work: "I have not reproduced [the Irish's] ingenuous insularity and [their] hospitality, the latter 'virtue' as far as I can see does not exist elsewhere in Europe."[4] Thus, even as ideal objective, the aim of satirical exposure premised on the theme of paralysis needs severe qualifications.

---

2. From a letter to Constantine Curran, August 1904; *Letters of James Joyce*, ed. Stuart Gilbert (New York: 1957), vol. 1, p. 55.
3. Cf. Florence L. Walzl, "Pattern of Paralysis in Joyce's *Dubliners*," *College English* 22 (1961): 221–28.
4. From a letter to Stanislaus Joyce, September 25, 1906, *Letters*, vol. 2, p. 166.

Joyce's intention to expose the spiritual decay of his countrymen and to caricature their afflicted souls was part of an attempt to set down a chapter in the moral history of his country. While he can ably defend his use of naturalistic details to dramatize inner conditions ("It is not my fault that the odour of ashpits and old weeds and offal hangs round my stories . . ."), he also feels justified in fashioning a "nicely polished looking glass" for reflecting the truth about life.[5] But Joyce never indulged in mere documentation, however sophisticated. If he chose Dublin as the setting of his stories "because that city seemed to me the centre of paralysis," or "the channel of poverty and inaction," he also believed that "the first step towards the liberation of my country" consisted in the capacity to face actuality without the screen of self-ingratiating illusions or sentimentality. A fidelity to experience is the prerequisite for cultivating honesty and awakening conscience. In creating the world of *Dubliners,* Joyce avoided equivocation: "I have written it for the most part in a style of scrupulous meanness and with the conviction that he is a very bold man who dares to alter in the presentment, still more to deform, whatever he has seen and heard."[6] Everything is judged by the artist in terms of the aesthetic ordonnance of the work itself; thus, in defending his use of the tabooed word "bloody," Joyce points out: "The word, the exact expression I have used, is in my opinion the one expression in the English language which can create on the reader the effect which I wish to create."[7]

It cannot, however, be completely denied that the persistent motif of spiritual disintegration recurs throughout *Dubliners* under various aspects and multiple disguises. For example, consider the "sense of a maleficent and

5. *Letters,* vol. 1, pp. 62–64, *passim.*
6. *Letters,* vol. 2, p. 134.
7. *Letters,* vol. 2, p. 136.

sinful being" personified by the priest in "The Sisters." Or take the insecurity and lack of communion in "Counterparts" or in "A Mother"; the despairing ordeals in "Eveline," "A Little Cloud," "A Painful Case"; the tormenting spirit of alienation pervading "The Dead." All the stories, in fact, testify to a predominantly moral vision which judges men in action. But one should not mistake this thematic preoccupation, the *donnée* of *Dubliners,* as proof of a didactic or tendentious motivation to instruct or convey precepts for good conduct. The measure of Joyce's moral vision lies ultimately in the quality, the depth and largeness, of our response to his rendition of characters and the world into which they breathe life.

May we say then, as many critics do, that the serious intent of the artist resides in the rhetorical and dramatic irony present in the conflict between individual aspirations or desires and the inauspicious barrenness of actuality? But irony is only part of the whole mode of representation, a stylistic feature controlled by the total effect the artist wants to produce. If one grants that irony provides the source of the organic, incremental disclosures in the plot which lead to "epiphany" in either the characters or the reader, then one can say that the theme of paralysis is subordinate to a larger, informing purpose: knowledge. For what good does any revelation serve except as a judgment of value, as an adequate illumination of its revealed object? Judgment leads to awareness of the knower, the known, and the relation between them. We easily understand this if we avoid identifying Joyce with any of his limited protagonists, even with Gabriel Conroy in "The Dead," and focus instead on the handling of action in the story—that is, on the whole dynamic complex of parts that include incident, character, thought, and diction.

Joyce the artist acts as the superintending consciousness which designs the whole form of the work, from beginning

to middle and end. Hence, to identify the artist with one
of his characters would be to destroy the integral connection between character and plot, character and thought,
and so on. In his reflections on aesthetics, Joyce insisted
on the supreme ideal of radiance, the perception of which
climaxes our understanding of the significance of the work.
Consequently, point of view and linguistic complications
turn out to be subordinate instrumentalities for achieving
the precise effect the artist wants.

Narrative form, to Joyce, represents the mode of art
"whereby the artist sets forth the image in mediate relation to himself and to others." Through his persona
Stephen Dedalus in *A Portrait of the Artist as a Young
Man,* Joyce elaborates on his idea of narrative form:

> The simplest epical form is seen emerging out of lyrical
> literature when the artist prolongs and broods upon himself
> as the center of an epical event and this form progresses
> till the centre of emotional gravity is equidistant from the
> artist himself and from others. The narrative is no longer
> purely personal. The personality of the artist passes into
> the narration itself, flowing round and round the persons
> and the action like a vital sea.[8]

One will perceive that it is narrative, not dramatic, form
that generates the proper aesthetic attitude of "stasis." In
Dubliners, the narrator throughout is not the incarnate
comic spirit who renounces any share in the world he
portrays; on the contrary, he is deeply concerned with
his characters, placing them in situations where we can
fully understand why they do certain things, for what

---

8. *A Portrait of the Artist as a Young Man,* ed. Chester G. Anderson
(New York: Viking Critical Library ed., 1964), pp. 214–15. For the pre-
ceding quotation on Joyce's view of narrative form, see Joyce's Paris
Notebook, entry dated March 6, 1903, in *The Workshop of Daedalus,* ed.
Robert Scholes and Richard M. Kain (Evanston, Ill.: Northwestern Uni-
versity Press, 1965), p. 54.

reasons and what ends. In other words, Joyce gives to his characters the integrity and vitality that the action of the story demands. We have working together in the narrative action both the objectivity of the critical intelligence and the identifying sympathy of the man behind the narrator, the incisiveness of analysis and the warmth of the creator. Realistic technique coalesces with the inner life of the imagination to produce Joyce's unique style.

The process of moving the "centre of emotional gravity" to a point equidistant from the artist himself and from others harmonizes with Joyce's three stages in the perception of beauty. In the first stage, the mind grasps the integrity of a work "when the aesthetic image is first luminously apprehended as self-bounded and self-contained." Fiction acquires wholeness or form by virtue of the principle that unites and organizes all the details in a particular order, treated in a manner so as to produce the requisite emotional effect. This principle inheres in the whole—completed and unified action so handled as to possess some particular emotional power.

In the second stage, the mind grasps the rhythm of the structure, the balance of part to part; "the synthesis of immediate perception is followed by the analysis of apprehension. . . . You apprehend [the thing] as complex, multiple, divisible, separable, made up of its parts, the results of its parts and their sum, harmonious."[9] Viewed in terms of the artistic product, the imaginative process of the artist is engaged in an analysis of the parts that will constitute the plot. The term *plot* as used in this study means—to use R. S. Crane's definition—"not merely a particular synthesis of particular materials of character, thought, and action, but such a synthesis endowed necessarily, because it imitates in words a sequence of human

---

9. *A Portrait of the Artist*, p. 212.

activities, with a power to affect our opinions and emotions in a certain way."[10] Put differently, the plot refers not to a mechanical concatenation of incidents moving toward a preconceived resolution, but a sequence of events defined by its specific moral and emotional movement so that this sequence determines what kind of effect the work will have. To determine the specific effect of a work, we have only to analyze the sequence. The chief problem for the artist, then, is the composition of parts, the adjustment of means to ends, in order to achieve a consonance necessary to arouse the desired responses.

In the third stage, the mind grasps the radiance of fiction when it cognizes how the plot is shaped in a way necessary to cause the emotional effects we get in reading, inasmuch as the production of these effects is the ultimate determinant of a story's form. The plot in effect embodies the power, interest, and feeling of a story.

Transposing the operations of the intellect to the realm of *poiesis,* the making of an artifice, we see how the form of fiction in *Dubliners* demonstrates the confluence of the three acts of the mind posited by Joyce to account for the experience of beauty. The radiance of a work springs from the proper ordering of the parts into a complex integral whole. When we perceive the necessary connections of incident and character in a story, the strict causal nexus of the parts, we move from the analysis of parts to an instant comprehension of the synthesizing principle of action. We then reach the final level of understanding: *claritas.*

The beauty of an artistic work, for Joyce, is "beheld by the imagination which is appeased by the satisfying relations of the sensible," while "truth is beheld by the intellect which is appeased by the most satisfying relations

10. "The Concept of Plot and the Plot of *Tom Jones,*" *Critics and Criticism Ancient and Modern*, ed. R. S. Crane (Chicago & London: University of Chicago Press, 1952) , p. 621.

of the intelligible."[11] In *Dubliners,* we find the sensible
and the intelligible fused together in the action of each
story. While the sensible and concrete particulars of incidents and characters exhibit the moral worth of the
agents and thus determine the affective meaning of the
action, the intelligible patterns may be discerned in the
series of happenings where characters undergo changes in
fortune, habit, or thought. The intelligible also includes
the inferences we draw in defining the purposeful continuity of the plot. In both character and plot, we see the
combination of the sensible and the intelligible operating
in harmony. For characters possess affective significance
or emotional charge when the specific choices and actions
unfolded in the plot reveal their moral nature. Such
revelations are indeed occasioned by, and at the same time
constitute, the plot defined as the sequence of probable
incidents which effect some important change (or reiterate
a habitual choice) in the protagonist, exhibiting a power
to move our emotions in a specific way.

The stories in *Dubliners* may then be interpreted meaningfully as imitations of actions rather than as exempla
or impressionistic sketches designed to indulge our sentiments or persuade us to approve or disapprove of certain
actions. In each story, we see a sequence of incidents
arranged in such a manner as to produce certain thoughts
and feelings in us. And it is through the deliberate arrangement of the incidents that we feel the power of
the narration and apprehend the form of the experience
being represented, its magnitude and seriousness. The
structure of the experience coincides with the plot, with
the pattern of causes and effects whereby a change in the
character's situation is gradually revealed. The characters
projected in the narrative, the agents whose actions are
seen to possess a determinate moral quality on which we

---

11. *A Portrait of the Artist,* p. 208.

pass judgment, are imitated mainly for the sake of the action. For nothing acquires moral or affective meaning unless it is attached to man as agent or man as possessing definite traits of character acting or being acted upon in situations determined by other agents. We can assert that it is the action that dictates the manner and realizes the purpose of the imitation. By the arrangement of incidents and character in a plot, fiction generates an epiphanic mode of recognition commensurate with the range and profundity of the moral vision informing the whole.

It is conceivable that Joyce, in spite of his Aristotelian inclinations, would dissent from the view that his stories can be labeled "imitations," especially since his notion of epiphany involves sudden psychic transformations. Moreover, his speculations on aesthetic purpose emphasize "stasis," arrest, rather than a dynamic interacting whole. But what are the stories in *Dubliners* if they are not imitations of actions? Did Joyce conceive moralizing arguments or symbolic discourses on despair, corruption, and other corollary themes? Would terms like *analogy, symbol,* and *myth* comprehend accurately the emotional and intellectual experience we have in reading the stories? Given the kind of fiction Joyce composed, narrative forms designed primarily to culminate in epiphanic insights, it might seem that the conception of a story as an imitation of action would be the opposite of what he had in mind.

We shall see, however, that in Joyce's thinking about art, the key word "epiphany" forms the essence of an imitated action. Epiphany means "showing forth," a recording of "a memorable phase of the mind itself." It denotes a transcript of a significant moment without any overt or direct commentary by the author. Joyce expressed the temporal scaffolding of epiphany thus:

> By an epiphany he meant a sudden spiritual manifestation, whether in the vulgarity of speech or of gesture or in a

memorable phase of the mind itself. He believed that it
was for the man of letters to record these epiphanies with
extreme care, seeing that they themselves are the most delicate and evanescent of moments. . . .

Imagine my glimpses of that clock as the gropings of a
spiritual eye which seeks to adjust its vision to an exact
focus. The moment the focus is reached the effect is epipha-
nized. It is just in this epiphany that I find the tried, the
supreme quality of beauty.[12]

Inspection of the epiphanies Joyce wrote will show that
they comprise incidents of varying length, or climactic
moments expressing the writer's thoughts or feelings
crystallized in vivid images. Epiphany may also refer to
the method of registering telling phenomena disposed in
a manner so as to perform the function of a "reversed
sign"—that is, a sign less informative of the external world
than connotative of the writer's mind. But the moments
of revelation never exist without an implicit narrative
base. Each epiphany implies a large enveloping incident
from which it derives sufficient import as a revelation of
"a memorable phase of the mind." Even when the
epiphany concerns a disclosure of an individual essence
by fortuitous means to a perceiving consciousness, still
it attains completeness when it is seen to form part of
the development of the whole action. Epiphany then acquires full import as a function of a larger action or
activity, whether implicit or explicit, in which a change
occurs. Its psychological appeal derives from the cumulative working of the whole system.

Epiphany also signifies *quidditas,* the whatness of a
thing, which is equivalent to *claritas,* the third stage of
aesthetic apprehension. It denotes the radiance of art. In
contrast to the concept of epiphany as the spiritual manifestation of the mind, Joyce defines epiphany in *Stephen*

12. *Stephen Hero,* ed. Theodore Spencer (New York: New Directions,
1944, reissue 1963), p. 211.

Hero as the quality of the aesthetic object when it reveals its wholeness and proportion, leading to a grasp of its radiance:

> *Claritas* is *quidditas*. After the analysis which discovers the second quality the mind makes the only logically possible synthesis and discovers the third quality. This is the moment which I call epiphany. First we recognise that the object is *one* integral thing, then we recognise that it is an organized composite structure, a thing in fact: finally, when the relation of the parts is exquisite, when the parts are adjusted to the special point, we recognise that it is *that* thing which it is. Its soul, its whatness, leaps to us from the vestment of its appearance. The soul of the commonest object, the structure of which is so adjusted, seems to us radiant. The object achieves its epiphany.[13]

In the context of the structure of incidents which we designate by plot, epiphany functions as a property of an incident that may be precisely located at the moment of reversal, when the character recognizes the meaning of something he has done or something that has happened to him as either in conformity with, or in opposition to, what he intended. In "The Dead," for example, Gabriel Conroy, upon learning of Gretta's early passion, gains an understanding of the reason behind, and the appropriateness of, the preceding events. This understanding generates thoughts and feelings that enhance his awareness. The protagonist receives a "spiritual manifestation" of events in that sequence, of the forces that motivate them, and of their probable continuity—the consonance of parts, the necessary progression from beginning to middle and end. Joyce was intent on creating form, not simply grouping constatations of epiphanic instants. He was trying to imitate actions. And the concept of action should be

13. *Ibid.*, p. 213.

carefully dissociated from theme, fable, argument, even
from the manifold parts of which it is composed.

The power of fiction to affect us involves its *claritas*
or radiance present in the mind as "the luminous silent
stasis of aesthetic pleasure." It inheres in the subtle adjustment of purpose, shape, manner, and material of the
mimetic process. What Joyce imitates in *Dubliners* are
actions (or activities) whose participants are chiefly middle-class or often lower-middle-class citizens whose deficiencies rank them below us, or alienate our sympathies.
The discord in the characters usually reflects some dis-
junction or conflict between consciousness and actuality.
Differences of actions (or activities) make for differences
of the agents required to give moral determination to
each incident in the plot embodying the action.

In accord with Joyce's aesthetic theory, the purpose in
presenting characters who are not heroic—that is, characters not as they are thought to be, not as they ought to
be, but as they are—is to bring about an equipoise of the
emotions. In a majority of the characters in *Dubliners,*
we find the coexistence of vices and redeeming virtues in
different proportions. If Joyce's purpose is to define character as a mean, a precarious existence between idealizing
spirit and circumscribing fact in a sequence of incidents
showing their defects and assets, what is then appropriate
would be language (diction, rhythm, etc.) fit to express
the clash and interplay of those forces. The manner of
representation—the scale and idiom of scenes, dialogue,
setting, thought (the power of saying whatever is appropriate to the occasion) —is determined by the object imitated. The phrase "scrupulous meanness" perfectly characterizes the manner of representation in *Dubliners,* which
consists of a nuanced alternation of objective description
and meditative lyricism, of analytic summary and allusive
texture.

In terms of Joyce's concentration on incidents demonstrating the defeat of will or on incidents where contingent
facts belie the dreams of the protagonist, the double-edged
signification of the term *epicleti,* which Joyce once used
to describe his stories, seems more appropriate than
epiphany in describing the precise emotional response he
strove to arouse. For *epicleti* refers not only to an invocation to the Holy Ghost in transubstantiating matter into
spirit; it also refers to a reproach or an imputation
(*epiklesis*). The people in *Dubliners* become the epicleti,
the accused summoned to stand trial to be judged for
what they are.[14] And Joyce's office is to render justice
tempered with sympathy.

---

14. See Robert Scholes and A. Walton Litz, eds., *Dubliners,* pp. 255–56.

James Joyce
and the
Craft of Fiction

Death mask of James Joyce

Part I
The Interpretation of Signs

1

THE SISTERS

THE INTRIGUING RIDDLE OFFERED US BY THE MOVEMENT OF incidents in "The Sisters" provokes inquiry into what causes the story to hang together and convey a powerful criticism of life. Deciphering the signature of Joyce's complex art, we move from the formulation of abstract principles of fiction to the task of explication. Our concern will always be with artistic, formal wholes. Since any work of art must possess a wholeness of meaning, it must show this wholeness not in similitudes or metaphoric equivalences but primarily in the construction and arrangement of the incidents in the story and the kind of change depicted in the protagonist.

"The Sisters" ends with an enigma. Eliza plays the role of uttering the coda, the epilogue to a situation in which the boy's sensibility acts as the medium through which everything—the priest, the phenomenon of death, his relatives, and so on—acquires significance. The boy's narration furnishes clues to his developing personality. Although dominated by his particular dreams and his memory, both limited modes of understanding at his age (memory is limited to the duration of the boy's acquaintance with the priest; the dream's end is forever submerged), he can entertain disparate views. Through the boy as central intelligence, we hear Eliza, the priest's sister, voicing the public sentiment in her choral commentary: "So then, of course, when they saw that, that made them think that there was something gone wrong with him. . . ." This biographical fact, impersonally rendered, embodies the attitude of the "outsiders," that is, those who composed the search-party and people like old Cotter and the boy's Aunt and Uncle, who represent conventional society. If Father Flynn has committed a sin, it is neither simony nor any mysterious sacrilege, but an omission: his absence at the moment he was needed by a parishioner. His non-fulfillment of his obligation is cited: "So one night he was wanted for to go on a call and they couldn't find him anywhere." Whatever his alleged sexual perversity or secular misdemeanor, that is not centrally foregrounded in the boy's consciousness. The priest's disappearing act, his inability to heed his calling, presents itself with unequivocal clarity as the principal cause for his being retired. The cause of this omission is in turn deducible from his conduct before the boy and the boy's perplexed response to his intellectual powers.

The illumination of complex reality—and the initially obscure details contribute to our heightened sense of recognition later—arises from the interaction of the inner realm of the boy's consciousness and the external world, the matter of empirical knowledge. William York Tindall points out the story's "static process of disclosure," in which the facts reach us chiefly through intermediary steps. Observations and notions are reported by the narrator. Because these modes of understanding reveal how the flux of experience affects the boy, his narration, both summary report and implicit comment, indicates that the action imitated by the plot involves the problem of showing the boy's break with his naïve trust in his illusory or subjectivized surroundings, as he proceeds to a conscious judgment of the differences between what is true and what merely appears convincing. Father Flynn, his absence becoming sheer presence to the boy, plays the role of mediator between mystery and opinion, between phenomenon and dream.

We observe that the boy's obsessive notion of "paralysis" when he reflects on the priest's withdrawal from contact manifests itself as the first sign of his maturity—his probing of reality by construing signs. He enters a sphere of indeterminacy, of being ill-at-ease in his world. The boy's groping self tends to interpret the world on the immediate sensory level. He is given to dreams and phantasies. Death, more specifically the priest's dying, strikes him at first as an inexplicable occurrence. His uncomprehending reaction to the word *paralysis* exhibits two antagonistic impulses that will characterize his assessment of his friendship with the priest:

> Every night as I gazed up at the window I said softly to myself the word *paralysis*. It had always sounded strangely in my ears, like the word *gnomon* in the Euclid and the word *simony* in the Catechism. But now it sounded to me like the name of some maleficent and sinful being. It filled me with fear, and yet I longed to be nearer to it and to look upon its deadly work.

The turnabout in his life is signaled by the words "But now. . . ." The boy is enormously interested in this destructive malady that has deprived him of his only intimate friend in the story.

The element of sound proves to be an enlightening clue to the tangled circumstances of Father Flynn's "sin." "Paralysis" is echoed by "sisters," and by a host of reverberating assonances: "Catechism," "sin," "chalice," "simony," "sipping," "coffined," "vicious," and so on. The catalogue can easily be multiplied to measure the range of semantic affinities, the cogency of which depends, as asserted above, on the sensory level of the boy's responses. The word *gnomon* (derived from Greek *gno-*, stem of *gignoskein*, to know), whose sound fascinates the boy, possesses the value of subtly connoting that the narrative progression of this story chooses the boy as point of view because it deals essentially with a youth's organic or plastic modes of knowing.

Father Flynn may be considered the *gnomon* in the narrative, a gnomon being defined as a geometrical figure that remains after a parallelogram has been removed from the corner of a similar but larger parallelogram. The removed parallelogram may refer to the boy's withdrawn admiration for him as he is chastened by what he learns later, or it may refer to the flaw, a loss of will, which rendered Father Flynn unfit to fulfill his duties. This flaw causes the accidental breaking of the chalice and his subsequent retirement. Although Father Flynn never appears in the story alive, he dominates the thoughts of everyone, in particular the boy's. Like a sundial's gnomon, which indicates time by the shadow it casts, the priest reveals the time or period of the boy's awakening to a free, independent life.

In death, then, Father Flynn casts a shadow on the boy in figurative and literal senses: the boy experiences a double mood: "I found it strange that neither I nor the day seemed in a mourning mood and I felt even annoyed at discovering in myself a sensation of freedom as if I had been freed from something by his death." Habitual expectations are not felt; and this reflection on a sharp discrepancy of landscape and psyche separates him from his naïve self and gives him a sense of liberation. Yet he is most sympathetic to the priest, as evinced by his anger toward old Cotter's innuendos. His nostalgic recollection of his past dealings with the priest, vividly described, supports his impartial authority as point of view in judging the priest's case. Thus, although removed from the stage of practical life, the dead priest seems to exert a stronger influence on the boy who, as the participating narrator, resurrects him in memory.

Given the data about the priest's failure to fulfill his vocation, does his stature in the mind of the narrator then dwindle? We can perceive that despite the boy's absorption of the facts, the priest's kind, venerable figure evoked in memory and dream will preserve its wholeness. Both his defects and virtues are given weight in the narrator's final reckoning. At the third stroke, no hope then remained for him except the hope of receiving vindication in the boy's heart.

Father Flynn's image displays an ambivalent cast relative to the boy and the other characters. To old Cotter and the sisters, Father Flynn became hopelessly insane; to the boy, he proved helpful and generous. The boy's predicament then lies in how to exercise discrimination in assessing facts, how to reconcile the two antithetical realms of public opinion and private conception.

As the plot unfolds, we recognize the priest's life as an example of how the paralyzing world of institutions can distort the will and damage the spirit. Bodily illness brought about by mental reservations and doubts further leads to the deterioration of the mind, the loss of balance. It would be absurd to insist on an exact correspondence of the gnomon's attributes and Father Flynn's image.[1] The structure of the story engages us with the kind of self-definition the event of the priest's death imposes on the growing boy through disclosing the gap between the order of the spirit and intellect and the order of the body subject to disease, insanity, and death. The boy's experience shows

---

1. Thomas E. Connolly describes the priest as having become "a re-mainder after something else has been removed"; "Joyce's 'The Sisters': A Pennyworth of Snuff," *College English* 27 (1965) : 195. See the objections to Connolly's literal reading made by Bernard Benstock, " 'The Sisters' and the Critics," *James Joyce Quarterly* 4 (Fall 1966) : 32-35.

how the priest and his peculiar misfortune aid him in
maturing toward a correct elucidation of the conflicting
powers of social norm and personal sentiment.

This disclosure of life's complexity by the event of death
acquires dramatic objectification in Joyce's expert handling of scenes. The movement from the outside to the
inside, from survey of the house's façade to the confrontation with the corpse, dramatizes the process of the boy's
maturation from mechanical knowledge of custom ("I
knew that two candles . . .") to knowledge of his own
nature. At the outset, the "lighted square of window"
could become meaningful to the boy who eagerly waits
to catch the "reflection of candles on the darkened blind."
Like the protagonist in "Araby," he must train himself
to read signs accurately. He notes then that the sensory
appeal of the landscape belies the demand for mourning.
So far, knowledge is mediated by limited circumstances.
For example, the news of the priest's death, a crucial
matter for his only close friend, reaches the boy not
through any "manifestation" in the window but through
old Cotter's mouth, the least congenial bearer of such
tidings. The next morning the boy gets a confirmation
of the news by the card in front of the shop.

Death to the boy assumes concrete lineaments in the
"heavy grey face of the paralytic," at which he drew the
blankets over his head "and tried to think of Christmas."
He learns, however, that fancy cannot dismiss the haunt-
ing impression of actuality. We recall the torpid man's
faded garments and his blackened handkerchief as we
note the boy's concealing act. The imagery of veiling or
concealing links with the *Drapery Shop,* with the window
blinds that bar the truth, with the screen of the confessional. In place of the ordinary sign "Umbrellas Re-
Covered," the obituary appears—a hint both ironic and
straightforward. Nobody can bring the priest back to life,
but his integral self can be recovered or reconstituted—

which is what the boy elegiacally does. In effect, the covering of innocence is snatched away before the unadorned finality of death. These images emphasize the boy's preoccupation with seeing, discovering, knowing.

We may also remark that the quality of vagueness and the "unassuming" look of the shop suggest the still blurred image of the priest, a composite of surface and depth, until the boy begins to recollect his past acquaintance with the dead. In his reminiscence, we see the priest solicit awed attention, his smile arousing a repulsion dissolved by closer acquaintance. The contrasting responses of repulsion and attraction are resolved in the summarizing phrase about the corpse's look: "solemn and truculent."

The first part of the boy's dream, a journey of the soul to "some pleasant and vicious region," reverses the pattern of responsibility when the boy absolves the priest—a gesture of his affection. Later, in daylight, he arrives at an intermediate awareness of his nature, resolving by juxtaposition his fear and love for Father Flynn: old Cotter's words revive the urge to remember the second part of the dream only to lead him to actuality. This transit from absorption in the subjectivity of dreams toward greater recording of actuality is fundamentally the abstract rationale or argument of the plot.

Of great significance is the shift in the boy's consciousness from the malicious Cotter to the exotic decor of the dream until subliminal fantasy gives way to the impact of the external world. The long velvet curtains, the swinging antique lamp, and strange Persian customs that surround his inward exploration (a parallel to the priest's retreat into insentience) seem to coincide with the houses of mourning that "looked to the west and reflected the tawny gold of a great bank of clouds." The boy's keen senses blend inner and outer realms in one dazzling procession. Finally the premonition of entering a veiled sanctuary, which the dream fails to realize, is realized

when the boy is ushered into the dead-room. Knowledge
by speculation is soon verified by the perception of the
link between observed event and observing sensibility:
"The room through the lace end of the blind was suffused
with dusky golden light amid which the candles looked
like pale thin flames." If the boy could not remember
the end of his dream, it is because Joyce wants to divert
the boy's consciousness from dream to objective life. The
movement of the plot itself charts the progress from dream
and memory to the concrete notation of what is actually
happening and thus provides the key to the meaning of
"The Sisters."

The action of the story embodied in the plot moves
from unquestioning impressions and haphazard notions
to the reporting of dialogue among adults (between Cotter
and the boy's guardians) and then to recollection. Impression and incident combined together reveal the uneasy
conflict between the boy's attachment to the priest and
his sense of liberation at his death. They also reveal the
tension between the Aunt's evaluation of the priest as a
"disappointed man" and the boy's liking for him as a
benevolent and tolerant mentor. The boy assumes the
role of priest-confessor in his dream, showing his respect-
ful and admiring regard for a man who, he thought, had
courage to perform the grave duties of his office. But his
admiration seems founded on a mistake, for he learns
later that the priest failed to pursue the grave duties of
his office.

Whether a surrogate for a decadent church or an impotent ogre, Father Flynn serves to join the inner and
outer facts of the boy's experience. On one level he
bridges the temporal and the spiritual; his death enhances
the slow birth of the boy's awareness engendered by his
growth away from the unthinking, habitual union with
his surroundings. What the narrative features here is not
the boy's violent reaction to death or his calm, detached

reporting, but his wrestling with the discrepancy between his feelings and the behavior of others toward the single incident of Father Flynn's death. The priest's dedication to the Cross and his failure to maintain it aptly justify Eliza's comment that his "life was crossed." But the idea of interchange or reciprocity latent in selfless devotion reinforces his function for the boy as mediating force or agent between what actually exists and what is simply thought.

Old Cotter's conversation affords a means of illustrating the boy's apprehension of the discord between himself and the people around him. We can take the suspended resolutions of the old man's sentences as correlatives to the boy's hesitant passage to maturity, further reinforced by such details as the priest's accident that disrupts Mass, his unfulfilled desire to visit his birthplace, and the like. That stylistic feature of incomplete predication recurs in Eliza's talk, inducing the boy to work out for himself the full context of those knowing hints. Old Cotter's "faints," the diluted impure spirit in distillation, suggests what is happening in the boy's psyche. His education begins right at the moment when he can detect and discriminate nuances in his response to people: "Though I was angry with old Cotter for alluding to me as a child, I puzzled my head to extract meaning from his unfinished sentences." The protagonists of the first three stories in *Dubliners* aggravate their difficulties because of their refusal to admit that they are still children even when they are growing up. Unable to extract or distill meaning from the talk of grown-ups, the boy nonetheless drinks the wine at the priest's wake—perhaps a proof of his having earned the privilege to join the adult world of ceremony and calculation.

The boy's confrontation with death and the revelation of a hidden fact (not the whole truth) about Father Flynn run against old Cotter's wayward aspersions. His calumny

against the priest's personality and his prejudiced suspicions force the boy to scorn him and instead favor the
priest, while all the time he (the boy) keeps discreetly
quiet and circumspect. To old Cotter and the insensitive
adults like him, the enigmatic character of Father Flynn
seems totally inaccessible. Even in death, his remains, and,
indeed, his whole life, are corroded by the superficial and
conformist world of his sisters. With its conservative
judgments and its rigid norms to which people blindly
adhere, Dublin society can never "worm out" the secret
of the priest's life. Nor can it penetrate the boy's inner
world of trust, guileless innocence, and receptive openness which now precariously adjusts itself to the contingencies of life. This virtue of sensitivity, part of the
tough resilience of youth, is cloaked by the flat matter-of-
fact tone in the latter half of the narrative.

One may perceive in the boy's participation at the wake
a proof of his earnest fidelity to the goodness and integrity
of his friend. His final judgment of the priest's life will
be based, not on the impersonal norms of the sisters or
his aunt, but on his own feelings. He tasted his sherry
"under cover" of the silent, gloomy lull. The information
about the priest's lapse—"He was too scrupulous always"—
follows the boy's partaking of the wine. Although he is
distracted by the slovenly sisters and by harsh and painful
facts, the boy's sincerity enables him to attain in the end
a poise by which he can appreciate the reasons why the
old priest would appear not as a grotesque or hideous
gargoyle to strangers but "solemn and truculent in death."

Many critics have discussed how the pathetic behavior
of the sisters exemplifies the mechanical routine of society
which blunts the malignant horror of death and simplifies
what to the boy appears as a fearsome ordeal. But the
ordeal involves not the fact of death as such, but the
criticism of the priest's life judged in relation to the boy's
affection for him. We have noted how Father Flynn's

scholastic casuistry and intellectual labor, directly opposed
to the boy's trusting simplicity, may have undermined his
will to act in unquestioning faith and mute obedience—
hence, his breaking of the chalice. But the boy's experience
in the wake shows how traditional patterns of conduct
simultaneously inhibit and control feelings, giving his
irresolute and spontaneous will a pattern for meeting the
challenge of crisis, in particular the contradiction between
personal experience and the standards of society.

The title "The Sisters," referring to the ineffectual
sisters of Father Flynn, derives its rationale from Joyce's
intention of stressing common personal bonds and intimate relationships needed to bridge the gap between
young and old and to vitalize a society deprived of any
familial coherence. Witness the orphan-boy's distance from
his Aunt and Uncle, and his heightening alienation from
adult society. Whatever symbolic import may be assigned
to them, the sisters—the adults in general—function as
agents who prepare the boy's initiation. For their knowledge of the past, especially of Father Flynn's unfortunate
accident, qualifies the boy's speculations and endows his
spirit with complicating substance.

In retrospect, the priest's death affirms his living presence in the boy's consciousness. The dead man paradoxically guarantees the ascendancy of the vigorous youth
over the past, over traditional usages and unreasoning
habit. While the public consensus (voiced by Eliza) is
given the last say with its clumsy pedestrian tone, the
narrative style conveys a sensible, humane moderation
which discourages, if not tempers, the boy's nearly complete surrender to the father-figure of the priest, insuring
thus a future unshackled from his youthful, irrational
enthusiasms. This is needed because, in spite of Eliza's
derogatory remarks (and old Cotter's), the boy seems
dangerously possessed by the priest's dominating, "truculent" image even in death.

The subjective drama of the boy's growth in intuitive awareness can be clarified further by focusing on the last impression the boy receives as he modifies his own mental picture: "I knew that the old priest was lying still in his coffin as we had seen him, solemn and truculent in death, an idle chalice on his breast." Earlier, the boy describes the priest's face as he confronts the "beautiful corpse" (a phrase fusing changelessness and aesthetic decorum) thus: "There he lay, solemn and copious, vested as for the altar, his large hands loosely retaining a chalice." Replacing "copious" with "truculent," he registers his altered estimate of his friend after hearing Eliza's account of how the others, his superiors, condemned him to useless retirement. Though labeled queer and unbalanced, he did not seem resigned but "truculent," ferocious, as though delivering a warning or ultimatum to all honorable sympathizers. Could it be that it is precisely this recognition of the ambiguous intricacy of life, the delicately hazardous tension in human relations, that holds both the "solemn and truculent" firmly synthesized in the boy's consciousness? Amid the funereal silence, the image of Father Flynn's face, serenely composed yet also fierce and purposeful, intrudes as fit emblem of the artist's craftsmanship.

2

AN ENCOUNTER

LIKE "THE SISTERS," WHICH INTRODUCES THE THEME OF THE painful rite of passage to final acceptance of one's belonging to common humanity, "An Encounter" presents another episode of confrontation with truth, with authentic self. Current interpretations assume that the old man with bottle-green eyes whom the boys meet functions as a father-figure or a defunct god.[1] Shifting our interest to the action of the narrative, we will see that the grotesque "pervert" enacts a positive service in confirming the narrator's sense of identity in terms of a role agreed upon by two persons. Here the ability to sustain a contract or play a game according to the rules signifies maturity.

Toward the "old josser," the sinister representative of the adult world, the boy reacts in an ambivalent pattern. This dual response is composed of two oscillating attitudes: the attitude to ideas and ideals, and the attitude to the physical appearance of those who exist as totems of authority or vehicles of the norm. A clear example of this duality in thought and feeling may be perceived in the boy's intuitive sizing-up of the old man: "His attitude

---

1. For example, William York Tindall, *A Reader's Guide to James Joyce* (New York: Noonday Press, 1959), pp. 17–19.

on this point struck me as strangely liberal in a man of his age. In my heart I thought that what he said about boys and sweethearts was reasonable. But I disliked the words in his mouth and I wondered why he shivered once or twice as if he feared something or felt a sudden chill." This ambivalence also prevails in the protagonist of "The Sisters" when he reflects on his reaction to Father Flynn's death. This dichotomy of the narrator's self, prepared by his urge for adventure and independence, looks forward to the end of the story. After the man's "queer" conduct, we get a reversal and a resolution of conflicting forces in the boy's self: the boy notes that the man "seemed to have forgotten his recent liberalism."

The ending of the boy's adventure transforms the negative (in the sense of frightful) presence of the old man into something without which the enlargement of his consciousness in the act of charity and purgation of pride could not have been brought about in the given situation. Obviously the man's monologue about the pleasure-giving value of whipping boys horrifies the narrator. Desiring to behave like an adult, he pretends to be unaffected. This pretense, in consonance with his love of romantic escapades, enables him to "escape." But at the same time it also enables him to convert what is mere play, an artificial agreement between playmates to change their names, into a realized mode of reconciling what he feels and what he recognizes as actuality. Necessity compels pretense, and pretense confirms the truth about the narrator's self.

The protagonist's friend Mahony proves his trustworthiness: he answers to his false name. The protagonist's call for help embodies the discovery that he cannot live alone in self-sufficient isolation, that he needs the help of others. What the boy's dilemma indicates is the fact that the ritual of play guarantees social arrangements made on faith, on each man's trust of another's word, which sustains the

normal process of life. The thrust of the concluding
paragraphs conveys the experience of catharsis, restoring
to the protagonist his sense of proportion. Lest he betray
his agitation, he maintains a pretense of decorum until his
boyish sensibility leads him to a sincere admission of his
faults and limitations:

> I went up the slope calmly but my heart was beating quickly
> with fear that he would seize me by the ankles. When I
> reached the top of the slope I turned round and, without
> looking at him, called loudly across the field:
> "Murphy!"
> My voice had an accent of forced bravery in it and I was
> ashamed of my paltry stratagem. I had to call the name
> again before Mahony saw me and hallooed in answer. How
> my heart beat as he came running across the field to me!
> He ran as if to bring me aid. And I was penitent, for in
> my heart I had always despised him a little.

The last sentence of the story includes both a confession
of an error and a self-dispensed absolution.

Throughout the adventure, the protagonist never indicates any wholehearted recognition of Mahony as a real
person and intimate friend except when, through a false
name, he summons him in urgent need. Prior to his sense
of crisis, he is proud to take the commanding position:
for example, he dissuades Mahony from pursuing two
ragged boys. He decides for Mahony their return by train.
He does not make any effort to prevent the old man from
dissociating him from Mahony—in fact, he claims a false
superiority over his friend "Mahony asked why couldn't
boys read them—a question which agitated and pained me
because I was afraid the man would think I was as stupid
as Mahony." Despite this attitude of sham knowledge
about books, the protagonist finds community with
Mahony as his peer. Although he is attracted to the old
man, he affirms complicity with Mahony in a game to

deceive the old man after Mahony warns him that the man is a queer, perverted simpleton—perhaps a pederast.

The bond of mutual reliance between the two boys emphasizes by contrast the ugly distortions of the adult world. It establishes the organic worth of dream-work and fantasy as a valuable training for engagement in practical affairs. It inculcates obedience to a code. For childhood games manifest a structure and motivation analogous to that of social conventions, of makeshift deals and compromises among grown-ups. Satisfying the primitive desire for make-believe and giving release to the spontaneous energy of youth, the myth of the Wild West together with the boisterous fights (mock-battles to adults) the boys construct around the myth are wholly alien to the realm of prudential economy. The innocent frolics of the children take place in the evenings after school, in Joe Dillon's back garden and the loft of the stable. Freedom also acquires the romantic ambience and glamor superimposed on sordid settings, provoking in the players an exuberant and fierce gaiety opposed to "the peaceful odour of Mrs. Dillon" and her pious regimen. Ironically, Joe Dillon, enamored of Indian war-dances, "had a vocation for the priesthood."

Wild adventure, however, yields to conscience when Leo Dillon fails to honor the plan agreed upon of a "day's miching." It turns out that the passion for "unruliness" which unites the boys of different cultures and constitutions does not possess Leo Dillon as completely as it does Mahony and the protagonist. Leo Dillon breaks his promise to join his friends in truancy. His weakness of easily submitting to adult impositions is illustrated by his "confused puffy face" when rebuked by Father Butler for indulging in the *Halfpenny Marvel*. But the incident, the narrator says, "awakened one of my consciences." The Dillons, in short, belong to the depersonalizing realm of normal workaday society—a society serious in the study of Roman History and of compliance to duty. Father Butler's reading of the first sentence in the history lesson, "Hardly had the day dawned . . . ," suggests the force of constraint, the spirit of discipline governing any endeavor to know or enact one's will.

To our protagonist-narrator, the scene in school intensifies the urge to escape confinement and decide for himself through a conscious commitment to action what his life should be. The choice of freedom, circumventing dutiful submission to authority, begins the drama of initiation consisting of the trip to the Pigeon House and the crucial encounter with the "green-eyed" man and the chastening of the protagonist's self-centered pose. Responsibility calls for response. The boy struggles to educate his own sensibility, shaping it in conformity with the ego's finitude, its fears and doubts and uncertainties.

The subjective motivation of the narrative development is furnished by the boy's growing unrest with his childhood milieu, his longing for escape, his fascination with the Wild West and with detective stories portraying "unkempt fierce and beautiful girls." Temporarily dismayed by the craven recoil of Leo Dillon before Father Butler's scolding, the protagonist finally resolves the impasse of mere daydreaming:

> But when the restraining influence of the school was at a distance I began to hunger again for wild sensations, for the escape which those chronicles of disorder alone seemed to offer me. The mimic warfare of the evening became at last as wearisome to me as the routine of school in the morning because I wanted real adventures to happen to myself. But real adventures, I reflected, do not happen to people who remain at home: they must be sought abroad.

The phrase "must be sought" and the tone of willed consent to experience disclose the impulsive desire of the protagonist to break the barriers between youth and maturity by a single gesture of determination.

If the education of the childhood ego requires the violation of the routine course of school, the agreement struck up among the truants can be fulfilled only by an evasive, necessary lie. The protagonist consigns his books to "the ashpit at the end of the garden," forsaking the fanciful stage of his mythical adventures for a real engagement. He sees the concrete external world with honest insight and keen sensitivity: "I sat up on the coping of the bridge admiring my frail canvas shoes which I had diligently pipeclayed overnight and watching the docile horses pulling a tramload of business people up the hill." Unlike that of the horses, the boy's spirit is intractable. The world is reborn to his senses; he feels his surroundings with a live intimacy so that as he surveys the world a concord of reality and consciousness seems spontaneously to emerge.

Mahony appears with a catapult, evoking at once an image of playful aggressiveness. His use of slang accentuates the disparity between the respectable middle-class boy and the outsider. Leo Dillon, failing to keep his promise, represents the comfortable creature of habit who paradoxically breaks his promise. He has "funked" the game; he has in this context shirked his responsibility to his peers.

The plight of the two adventurers signifies an immersion in the world of facts: "the spectacle of Dublin's commerce," the ferryboat and the Norwegian vessel in which the narrator fails to see a foreign sailor with "green eyes." Unable to decipher the legend on the vessel, he examines the sailor's eyes and hears the assuring voice of a tall man: "All right! All right!" Is everything all right in the world of work? Is the boys' truancy "all right" to the elders of society?

No hindrance or obstacle presents itself to the boys

until the appearance of the old "josser." They roam around the slum area of Ringsend, buying food from the shops there, accepting its squalor and adapting themselves to the environment as though their games in the stable and the garden of their fancied Wild West had oriented them to the dirt and misery of the place. With fatigue and the lateness of the hour, they abandon their original project of visiting the Pigeon House (symbolic, to many commentators, of Irish frustration and sacrilege).[2] But although the original goal is not reached, somehow the fortuitous meeting with the old man turns out to be the inevitable and necessary climax to the protagonist's adventure. In effect, the boys' aimless wandering has not diverted them from achieving the purpose of their quest—to prove their fitness in setting forth without adult assistance or supervision and in learning to adjust to the demands of actuality.

The whole experience of escape from school justifies itself in the confrontation with menacing reality as personified by the old "josser." Whatever symbolic content or implication may be discerned in the figure of the old man, the unquestionable fact is that he jolts the protagonist into an awareness of his futile pretensions and his need for the comfort of his friend.

Within the framework of the narrative action, the old man acquires value as a means of initiating the boy into a discovery of his true self by a reversal of his own feelings and expectations. The old man exhibits a peculiar mixture of polite culture and sadistic cruelty; he typifies the civilized world which pays for the price of refinement by unnaturally deforming the erotic impulses for the maintenance and preservation of social order. The erotic potencies of personal attachments, pleasure, and pain subsist together in the expression of the concealed, darker

---

2. See Marvin Magalaner and Richard M. Kain, *Joyce The Man, the Work, the Reputation* (New York: New York University Press, 1956; reissue 1962), pp. 86–88.

side of man's complex nature as illustrated by the old man. The man's fixation on whipping boys, his obsession with this violent release of perverse impulse, impresses the boy as if it were "some elaborate mystery," while the man's voice "grew almost affectionate and seemed to plead with me that I should understand him." The world of inhibited man craves understanding and sympathy from the unspoiled youth. But the protagonist's instinct, gifted with discerning cautiousness that constitutes his saving grace, apprehends the threat in the pervert's insistence because the boy himself possesses an equivalent measure of pride. This pride coincides with the assertion of initiative and individuality which leads paradoxically to his denial of the man's solicitation and his affirmation of solidarity with his peer. The protagonist's fright arouses a need for the other person, for Mahony, the aimless but unpretentious friend, and defines his character as "penitent" for his errors of judgment.

Counterpointing his humiliation, the self-awareness gained by the protagonist in the end evolves from his triumphant, self-confident happiness in the beginning to the moment he flees the man by climbing to the top of the slope from which he could call Mahony. He fears the destruction of his integrity, seized by the apprehension of the truth that, for one thing, the notion of "green eyes" belonging to fabulous sailors turns out to be the attribute of a man who delights in torturing boys. His fear that the man will injure him reveals that his youthful self, seeing how romantic sentiments and dreams can be distorted by actuality, still possesses the capacity to redeem its own defect. Our sympathy for the protagonist is heightened by our inference that he suffers a painful renunciation of his premature claims to proud individuality, yet at the same time he progresses to the level of maturity he had earlier feigned.

In what manner does the danger posed by the old man

strike the boy? Apart from his physical ugliness, the "great gaps in his mouth between his yellow teeth," the moral deformation of the old man betrays itself in the weird monotone and hypnotic style of his utterances. The manner and substance of his monologue suggest a paralytic reflex, an automatism which isolates the mind in a vacuum and exacerbates the instinct of exercising absolute power and discharging sadistic lust. The ritual of whipping imaged by his utterances evokes profound conflict in the boy's self, for earlier he was both attracted to and repelled by the old man.

The old man as an example of the mature adult frightens the boy and congeals his spirit. The circular movement of the old man's utterance seems to weave a snare around the protagonist, whose strongest impulse is to break out of the repetitious, circular impotence of daily existence. The boy sensitively records the speaker's concentration on "chastising boys," his guilt condemning him to impoverished solitude. Evading the subtle entanglement of degraded habit and depraved custom, the protagonist learns the ultimate absurdity of personal freedom used for selfish enjoyment and release of impulses not satisfied by the normal experience of daily life. He chooses respect for the other person's (Mahony's) integrity, and thus accedes to the obligation of being true to a dominant part of his own self which he finally confronts— the proud, selfish, and wild adventurer seeking indulgence for his whims and fancies. The protagonist at the end finally learns the wages of experience and assumes the new role of a man who, knowing the limits of freedom and personal will, struggles to test his private thoughts and feelings in confrontation with the cruel ironies of ordinary existence.

3

ARABY

AMONG THE VARIOUS REASONS WHY THE EXISTING INTERPRE-
tations of "Araby" have failed to grasp the principle of
organization informing the narrative, I would point to the
wrong emphasis placed upon stylistic details—the texture
of description, the rhetorical appeals of imagery and ambiguous allusions, symbols, and so on—and the distortion
of form created by this emphasis.[1] For if the formal whole
of the story resides in the parts, the verbal devices which

---

1. This essay assumes the relevance and qualified validity of all the
existing interpretations of "Araby." Confining myself strictly to a description of the structure of the plot and its function in determining the
whole narrative action, I thus inquire—if my description is correct—into
the premise or condition whereby any other evaluation of details would
be considered valid or consistent with the larger subsuming structure.
I therefore assume here the Aristotelian position regarding the primacy
of plot in mimetic art. For the elaboration of motifs and themes in the
story, and their relation with Joyce's achievement, I refer the reader to
the following works: Bernard Benstock, "Arabesques: Third Position of
Concord," *James Joyce Quarterly* 5 (Fall 1967) : 30–39; Harry Stone,
" 'Araby' and the Writings of James Joyce," *Antioch Review* 25 (Fall
1965) : 375–410; Robert P. Roberts, " 'Araby' and the Palimpsest of Criticism, or Through a Glass Eye Darkly," *Antioch Review* 26 (Winter 1966–
67) : 469–89; William York Tindall, *A Reader's Guide to James Joyce*
(New York: Noonday Press, 1959), pp. 19–21; Marvin Magalaner, *Time
of Apprenticeship: The Fiction of Young James Joyce* (New York: Abelard-Schuman, 1959), pp. 79, 87, 101; James A. Fuller, "A Note on
Joyce's 'Araby,' " *CEA Critic* 20 (February 1958) : 8.

constitute the means of representation, then we may ask
why the narrative has to present events in a sequence.
And why should such an experience, consisting not only of
images or of thoughts but also of decisions leading to acts
that change the situation of the protagonist—why should
the boy's experience be arranged in the precise order of
revelation that we find in the story?

We can clearly account for the kind of formal wholeness realized by the story if, assuming that the whole is
composed of a meaningful sequence of parts, we can
formulate the principle enabling the story to exercise its
power upon us through its own aesthetic integrity. My
concern then would be with the formal structure of the
story, the disposition of parts—plot, character, thought,
and diction—in order to achieve certain effects.

The plot of "Araby" is a dynamic and complex one,
consisting of a change in the fortune of the protagonist
from a passionate "lover," sensitive and obsessed with
heroic possibilities, to a disappointed visitor of a bazaar.
Put this way, one perceives the absence of any contradiction between the initial condition and the final state of
the character. A reversal occurs on the level of expectation
and its nonfulfillment: the boy promised Mangan's sister
to bring her a gift if he should succeed in going to the
bazaar. The conditional mode of expressing his intention
clearly discounts any exaggerated vision of future accomplishment; but this effect is part of the marked contrast
in tone between the dialogue and the emotional response
surrounding this isolated exchange between the idolized
girl and the idealizing sensibility of the boy:

—It's well for you, she said.
—If I go, I said, I will bring you something.
What innumerable follies laid waste my waking and sleeping
thoughts after that evening!

and so on. Note the similar discrepancy, the curve of

deflation, in the preceding paragraphs, with the paragraph
beginning "One evening I went into the back drawing-
room. . . ." That isolation, the feeling of acute empathy,
accelerates into sublime rapture, only to be undercut by
the factual transcript of the first verbal exchange:

> All my senses seemed to desire to veil themselves and, feeling
> that I was about to slip from them, I pressed the palms of
> my hands together until they trembled, murmuring: "O love!
> O love!" many times.
>   At last she spoke to me. When she addressed the first words
> to me I was so confused that I did not know what to answer.
> She asked me was I going to *Araby*. I forgot whether I an-
> swered yes or no. It would be a splendid bazaar, she said
> she would love to go.

The nature of the boy's response provides a key to our
understanding of why the experience in the bazaar should
be an inevitable conclusion and the last statement a surprising but probable generalization of the boy's ordeal
for himself.

We derive quite a different perception of the boy's predicament, a grasp of the limitations and possibilities of the
epiphany uttered at the end, in our acquaintance with the
movement of the plot. The action proper begins with the
middle of the story, with the paragraph beginning "At
last she spoke to me. . . ." Prior to this, the exposition
gives us all the relevant facts and information needed to
make the boy's actions most probable and his response
both unexpected and most likely. An inverted-pyramid
pattern holds the details of setting (from panoramic scope
to gradual localization into scenic background: North
Richmond Street to garden and drawing-room, etc.) , of
space and time, until, the external circumstances established, the boy's inner world is systematically disclosed,
from past routine—the collective sharing of childhood
games in habitual times and places—to emotional concen-

tration on his affection for Mangan's sister. Then, with the interiorization of this particular person in the boy's consciousness, the narrator describes what consequences arose from this focus on her image, how the world's appearance varied, how the boy's attitudes and feelings toward his habitual ways and associations subsequently changed, until his commitment to a promise moves him to action. The order of the exposition is controlled by a rhetorical purpose: to arouse our sympathetic identification with the boy by a vivid, concrete actualization of his world in sensuous details and their appeal to the boy's awareness of value at this stage. Thus the objective recording of surface phenomena—houses with "brown imperturbable faces," "musty" air of the drawing room, curled and damp pages of books, and the like—entails the corresponding effects on the boy's mind implied by the emphasis on sensory qualities: visual, auditory, tactile, and olfactory sensations predominate.

As the exposition develops, the stages of temporal specification harmonize with the concurrent heightening of the boy's presence in such an environment. Environment becomes a world. The first two paragraphs consist of the general and the particular geography of the story; the next two paragraphs convey the general (season) and specific temporal duration of the boy's experience prior to the momentous Saturday, the journey/pilgrimage to *Araby*. Further narrowing or close-up in time is accomplished by the change from the customary "Every morning I lay on the floor in the front parlour" to the climactic "One evening I went into the back drawing-room," this transition bridged by a paragraph embodying the charismatic force of the girl's image on the boy's consciousness, the cathexis of energy somehow converting the series of events in the boy's Saturday evenings into a static configuration. The total impact reduces his existence to a poetic instrument: ". . . my body was like a harp and her words

and gestures were like fingers running upon the wires."
The orientation of place and time functions chiefly to
form our idea of character in revealing the boy's thoughts,
ideas, attitudes, and feelings about the objects and persons
around him. Description of place contains within itself
the manner of perceiving and responding. The narrator
renders the boy's solidarity with his peers, their sense of
community and sportiveness, his awareness of affective
qualities, without discrimination:

> The space of sky above us was the colour of ever-changing
> violet and towards it the lamps of the street lifted their
> feeble lanterns. The cold air stung us and we played till
> our bodies glowed. Our shouts echoed in the silent street.
> The career of our play brought us through the dark muddy
> lanes behind the houses where we ran the gauntlet of the
> rough tribes from the cottages, to the back doors of the
> dark dripping gardens where odours arose from the ashpits,
> to the dark odorous stables where a coachman smoothed and
> combed the horse or shook music from the buckled harness.

Our inferences about the boy's character may be formulated in relation to what happens later, in terms of capacities to do certain things and to react in a certain way.

One major inference, quite apart from the boy's sensitive temperament and vigorous constitution, is his growing interest in the female sex as a class. Although the class
is here represented by Mangan's sister, the designation
itself seeks to preserve the generality to which the boy's
image of the girl conforms. Her "brown figure," her
"image," "her name," refuse to crystallize into any indi-
vidualized person. In fact, the two occasions in which the
boy apprehends her presence yield evidence for his tendency to introject, or internalize, what is observed. The
first description—"Her dress swung as she moved her body
and the soft rope of her hair tossed from side to side"—
brings about a rapturous and intensely idealized response

radically out of proportion to his slight acquaintance with the girl. Premised on this slight acquaintance, the boy naturally draws out of his inner resources (where religious, sexual, romantic imagery mix; the Tristan-Isolde romance and the cult of courtly love condense all these attributes) the force to endow her image with life. And the testimony of her life depends not on her actual existence, her reality as perceived, but on the quality of his response to her image, her reality as conceived. Obviously she, as intentional object of devotion, seems overdetermined: her image becomes a sacred "chalice" to the grail-hero.

Given this intense, passionate attraction to an idealized presence, we can understand his promise to bring a gift from *Araby* and his anxiety to perform the steps necessary to confirm his vow. But if the impetus to stylized worship gives strong, compelling direction to the boy's impulses and his irrational vitality in inventing fantasies, it also removes him farther and farther from ordinary life. Such indeed is the effect he records after the promise. But even before the promise is given, the boy has already exiled or cast himslf out from the vulgar and business world: recall his chivalric withdrawal as he walked through the "flaring streets."

This withdrawal from the ordinary world and the removal from the level of material circumstance, a logical result of the boy's concentration on his self-generated object of worship, serves to motivate his estrangement from his aunt and uncle, his anger at their unconcern, and his agonized yearning to reach the temple-like bazaar where he will finally obtain the "chalice" and thus fulfill the sacramental object of his quest. The reality of the "chalice" depends on his promise to bring back something. Mangan's sister acquires all sorts of religious associations in the course of time; likewise, the bazaar attracts all the energy of idealization the boy can sustain, his spirit inflamed by opposing forces. The feeling of frustration, anger, and despairing revolt that we see in the boy at the end can be comprehended only on the basis of these expectations.

But the concluding statement is not wholly that of the boy as narrator-participant; it is also properly that of himself as the adult narrator who is reconstructing an experience from which he is now detached in space and time. Since then, the narrator obviously has gained some knowledge of the world and of the complexity of life to be able to clarify the predicament of the boy in this meaningful way. Because of this peculiarity, the narrative exists on two planes: the boy-participant (an imaginative projection) and the narrator. The narrator is the central intelligence whose judgment of the boy's experience as he undergoes it is subtly fused with the structure of the plot and is, at many points, exposed by telling overt comment. Joyce's problem in composing "Araby" lies, I suggest, in contriving a method to combine the authoritative first-person account and the balanced poise of the narrator who has organized the account in precisely the order we have it. It is the old problem of reconciling the confessional, witnessing virtues of the first-person viewpoint with the rational distance and sense of the totality usually ascribed to the omniscient storyteller. As I have noted above, the style and tone of description is the mature narrator's, especially in conceptual treatment: "The other houses of the street, conscious of decent lives within them, gazed at one another with brown imperturbable faces." The animistic charge invested in the "face" of the houses manifests its continuity in the hostile aspect of *Café Chantant's* front: "I looked humbly at the great jars that stood like eastern guards at either side of the dark entrance to the stall."

Seen in the light of this ambiguous narrative voice, the conclusion may then be construed as a product of two lines of force, one dramatized in the progression of the

plot and the other implicit in all the opposing elements
that form the countermovement to the plot and thus constitute the agent of the reversal. The conclusion marks the
triumphant harmony of the two narrative spheres of subjective (sensory) experience and objective (conceptual)
understanding:

> Gazing up into the darkness I saw myself as a creature
> driven and derided by vanity; and my eyes burned with
> anguish and anger.

Ironically, this act of recognition is expressed as an act
of "gazing into the darkness," that is, a perception of
actuality: "the lights of the upper part of the hall had
been extinguished." Cognizing the external world, the
boy immediately becomes the mature narrator and recognizes his previous state. He executes this leap in the transi-
tive mode of separating what he was and what he is now;
and in producing a reflection of himself, one the seer and
the other the image of himself seen, he defines his situation by that metaphor of "reflection." The emotional implication of the concepts frees him from his mistake of
sentimental exaggeration; he objectifies the cause of the
mistake in the word "vanity." "Vanity" is the active force
that has led him to form undue expectations; "vanity" has
driven and derided him to that extreme, to the "darkness"
that is the end of his boyish indulgence. He is a "creature"
whose eyes, both the cause of the delusion and the libera-
tor from that delusion, "burned with anguish and anger"
—anguish at the sense of being responsible for his plight
and accepting it as such, anger at his "blindness" in not
realizing the nature of his plight. If the principle for the
shaping of the narrative is logically prior to the temporal
unfolding of the plot, then it remains now to trace how
the principle of organization implied in the concluding
statement guides the sequence of incidents and the cause-

effect relation among the different elements comprising such incidents.

"Vanity" is etymologically "empty," hence futile or blind. Negativity pervades the sense of place in the beginning: "blind" street, uninhabited house, hollow middle-class residences, empty drawing room, dead priest, decaying books, wild garden, straggling bushes, rusty bicycle pump, winter dusk, "dark muddy lanes," uncle, shadow, "back doors of the dark dripping gardens where odours arose from the ashpits," and "dark odorous stables." One can isolate the analogical matrix of "darkness," vanity, anger, and anguish of the last sentence in the imagery and the connotations of words that convey the relation of the boy to his world. With these realistic details, a few more reality-oriented judgments that one can ascribe to the mature narrator establish the counterforce to the idealizing tendency of the boy's passion and subsequently effect the reversal. (For even here one can see that the boy's connection with the world of squalor and vulgar indifference guarantees the firm, inescapable background for his existence in the world.) Consider these insinuated judgments:

> her name was like a summons to all my *foolish* blood.

> Her name sprang to my lips at moments in *strange* prayers and praises which *I myself did not understand.*

> My eyes were often full of tears (*I could not tell why*) and at times a flood from my heart *seemed* to pour itself out into my bosom. . . . *I did not know* whether I would ever speak to her or not or, if I spoke to her, how I could tell her of my *confused* adoration (*emphasis supplied.*)

Apart from the negative references to surroundings, the priest's dubious life, and the lack of visualized clarity in the girl's figure as apprehended by the boy, one detects the uncertainty undermining his irresistible passion for the girl's image in his mind. Indeed, his adoration is "confused," in both senses.

The boy's confusion, the chaotic and undefined response to the outside world at this stage of his experience, infects the first verbal contact between him and Mangan's sister. Note the failure of memory—the key to the reversal:

> At last she spoke to me. When she addressed the first words to me I was so confused that I did not know what to answer. She asked me was I going to *Araby*. I forgot whether I answered yes or no.

The boy's confusion and the failure of his memory foreshadow his fate at the bazaar. Becoming aware of her presence—severely qualified, selectively filtered to produce what many have considered a madonna image—and directly though mildly encouraged by her, he utters his crucial vow: "If I go, I will bring you something."

From this point, the movement gathers force in the direction of fulfilling the vow. But here the conflict between potent impulsive inwardness and the indifferent world grows sharp and almost dominates the foreground of the boy's consciousness. Owing to the strength of the distracting force exerted by the aunt, the master of the class, Mrs. Mercer, and the uncle, the boy's memory seriously suffers a fatal decline. At first he wanted to destroy outer reality: "What innumerable follies laid waste my waking and sleeping thoughts after that evening." But even as he wishes "to annihilate the tedious intervening days," he acknowledges his "follies." Immediately after confessing *Araby*'s "Eastern enchantment," he mentions his Aunt's reluctance, suspecting some "Freemason affair," his master's strictness and suspicion of idleness. How shall we take these next two utterances except as 1) the actual state of the boy-participant at the moment of experience, and 2) the depreciating comment of the mature narrator:

> I could not call my wandering thoughts together. I had
> hardly any patience with the serious work of life which, now
> that it stood between me and my desire, seemed to me
> child's play, ugly monotonous child's play.

Finally, the momentous day arrives—a transitional stage
from the end of the week, Saturday, to Sunday, the beginning of a new week, plus all other associations in Christian
liturgy. Every detail concerning the uncle's behavior—
fussing with hat-brush, his return at nine o'clock registered by the rocking of the hallstand as it receives the
weight of his overcoat—climaxed with his forgetting of the
boy's intention, works toward blocking the primary action
of the plot. Framed within the departure of the uncle and
his arrival, the boy's experience—his bad humor, his heart's
misgiving, his irritation—shows how time becomes human-
ized, a lived duration, measured in the stream-of-conscious-
ness. Not entirely, however, since the boy's almost complete engulfing by, and immersion in, clock-time is
avoided when he easily affirms his imaginative freedom
by going up to the "high cold empty gloomy rooms." The
epithets almost epitomize the whole course of the plot.
He stresses his alienation from the world outside, and in
the very process reveals to us (but unheeded by himself)
the cause of his temporary imbalance: the dangerous
prevalence of the imagination. It is his imagination that
affords life and value to Mangan's sister, not her real existence. Consequently, everything depends on the imagination, whose muse is memory:

> The high cold empty gloomy rooms liberated me and I went
> from room to room singing. From the front window I saw
> my companions playing below in the street. Their cries
> reached me weakened and indistinct and, leaning my fore-
> head against the cool glass, I looked over at the dark house

where she lived. I may have stood there for an hour, seeing nothing but the brown-clad figure cast by my imagination, touched discreetly by the lamplight at the curved neck, at the hand upon the railings and at the border below the dress.

That passage compresses the two occasions in the story where Mangan's sister is described.

When he goes downstairs, however, we realize that his imagination and its efficacy depend on the limitations of time and place, the specific locale of his existence. And this condition of his imagined passion he has not at all accepted as an *a priori* ground of experience. While his idealism may be qualified by his sharp observation of the world, the world presents itself as colored and transformed by the pressure of his emotions. Thus we note a foreshortening in the gap between desire and the fulfillment of desire which he envisions, anxious and angry at his uncle's dereliction and the joke of the verses "The Arab's Farewell to his Steed." But finally the florin—a big sum for him—reinforces the movement to the glamorized goal, the *Araby* of his imagination.

So far, we anticipate the trip to *Araby* in a general way, knowing the driving force of his affection for the girl. But he finds later that it was not affection but vanity that drove him. Having overcome the obstacle of the indifferent adults—the boy's orphanhood justifies his courage to initiate himself into experience and to seek for symbols of authority—he now seems headed for the successful accomplishment of his quest. But the development of the narrative continues to interweave with the surface-movement, the journey to *Araby*, the resisting force. Unable to prevent his departure from the house, this resisting force—call it the corrupt Mammon-worshiping world of reality, the paralyzed philistine public, or what you will—now accompanies the boy's trip as an ominous part of the environment. At first, environment vivifies memory, whose failure threatens to ruin the project of the imagination: "The sight of the streets thronged with buyers and glaring with gas recalled to me the purpose of my journey." But from then on, the details of awareness convey to us a meaning counter to the literal motion of events: third-class carriage of a deserted train, ruinous houses, and improvised wooden platform. The positive note, though present, is subdued: twinkling river, special train, lighted dial of a clock, magical name.

Before the boy overhears the conversation at the *Café Chantant,* we observe that the florin is split up and lowers in denomination. This dwindling of monetary value parallels the gradual destruction of any hope of buying a present. The boy feared that the bazaar would be closed; he sacrifices a shilling to enter his "magical" Castle Perilous. But the weary-looking man simply heralds more disillusioning aspects: closed stalls, dark hall. As a result of the boy's inability to summon up the girl's image, to clearly remember the reason for his trip, the world slowly encroaches upon his consciousness from the moment he enters *Araby.* Distracted by the fall of the coins, he sees two men counting money on a salver: "Remembering with difficulty why I had come I went over to one of the stalls and examined porcelain vases and flowered tea-sets." The frivolous rhythm of talk between men and lady about truth and falsehood, and the woman's unencouraging and dutiful tone, do not greatly differ from the recorded exchange between him and Mangan's sister. His reply to the lady, "No, thank you," simply punctuates his feeling of emptiness—the sense of vanity—registered by the material sound of his "two pennies falling against the sixpence" in his pocket. Victim of his bad memory (the Muse is memory herself), he is defeated by what he thought the world of *Araby* would be. Remembering the past clearly, the artist becomes the priest of his own sacrifice.

The pattern of emotional response outlined here by

pursuing the plot as it moves in one direction, either speeded up or impeded by the acts and responses of the protagonist, illumines finally the meaning of the epiphanic vision at the end. It is a conclusion for the primary plot involving the boy's quest and his journey to *Araby* on a metaphorical dimension; it is a conclusion, too, for the countermovement of the plot that involves the conditions which make the boy's quest probable at first, and improbable and thus "wonderful" (in Aristotle's sense) in the end. For the boy's character, right from the first paragraph, contains its own problem and solution. And the dialectical movement from problem to solution, rendered in the plot, obeys the principle of telling a story to achieve a difficult effect that is both paradoxical and ironic: the boy's experience—virtually an ordeal in the interpretation of signs—rendered at the moment of happening from a perspective of knowledge and just comprehension. The boy is aware of things but not the meaning of things; the narrator obliquely delivers the meaning of things to us. Interpreted in this way, one perceives "Araby" as Joyce's finest accomplishment in holding justice and reality in a single luminous imitation of an action.

Part II
A Special Odor

4

EVELINE

"EVELINE," THE FIRST STORY IN *Dubliners* TO NAME THE central personage with a single predicament, combines the principal thematic interests of the three preceding stories. Like the boy in "The Sisters," the central character feels the impact of death and the need to resolve the conflict of attitudes and sympathies within her. Eveline, like the proud adolescent of "An Encounter," realizes the danger of removing herself from the shelter of household pieties, and this realization overwhelms her until she is hopelessly paralyzed; yet she remains moored to the firm core of her motherly self. Like the questing hero in "Araby," she performs trivial but inherently symbolic tasks that make her plight at once concrete and universal: "Then she had to rush out as quickly as she could and do her marketing, holding her black leather purse tightly in her hand as she elbowed her way through the crowds and returning home late under her load of provisions."

Seen in the light of her horrified refusal to be "saved" by Frank at the end of the story, Eveline is a failed heroine. She assumes the guise of a protagonist-victim who nonetheless proves equal to the expectations of her society. She has struggled hard to "keep the house together," and to insure the young children's growth in their being properly fed and regularly sent to school. In fact, part of her failure to commit herself completely to Frank and what he stands for stems from her glimmering recognition in the early part of the story that, on balance, her life in Dublin was not so bad as it sometimes appeared: "It was hard work—a hard life—but now that she was about to leave it she did not find it a wholly undesirable life."

What makes her panicked recoil in the end lose its quality of abject and repulsive cowardice, attracting the reader's sympathy in turn, is the consistency of her portrayal as a woman whose response to life takes place on a basic, elemental plane. Her character is rendered in its receptive and engaging openness, her impressionable mind making her both a loving appraiser and an efficient instrumentality of her surroundings. Note her passive, immobile position depicted in the first paragraph: "She sat at the window watching the evening invade the avenue. Her head was leaned against the window curtains and in her nostrils was the odour of dusty cretonne. She was tired." She was tired, not so much of the dreary, sordid routine of her occupation, but of the household chores which she feels as physically exhausting labor. This fatigue is not peculiarly a symptom of revolt; indeed, revolt seems unlikely for a girl who, not yet over nineteen, perceives life in terms of something submitting, or someone overcoming something—as suggested by the gestural force of "invade," "lean," and the like.

One may perceive a pun on her name in the sound of "the evening invade the avenue." The past encroaches on and possesses her; in the grip of a dead past, surrounded by the funereal cretonne curtains and the futile, heavy dust, she can do nothing now but stay submerged in a double retreat of introspection and reminiscence. The description of her existence in time and place tallies with the recurrent image of drowning, or of being engulfed, which, in the last scene, literally muffles her into anguished paralysis. She registers sounds and odors with sensitive delicacy; the aural and visual sensations evoke scenes of the past in her memory.

These childhood experiences involve change in the physical environment and also mutation of the self. Recollection ushers a comparison with her present circumstance and leads into an ironic juxtaposition of herself in relation with past and present: "Everything changes. Now she was going to go away like the others, to leave her home." She does not really desire a change, in the radical sense of violent transposition; she wants a return of the warm security of her childhood and a recovery of her mother's protective care. Lacking that sense of comfort and the poise it gives, she herself seeks to fulfill the role of mother in her youthful way until the time when, introduced to Frank's romantic world, she allows her buried self—the innocent, primitive aspect—to exult in deceptive longings and dreams.

Recollecting her past, she reveals her latent fear of her father: "Her father used often to hunt them in out of the field with his blackthorn stick; but usually little Keogh used to keep *nix* and call out when he saw her father coming." Eveline's other self may be conceived a *nix,* which refers in Germanic mythology to a water sprite who sometimes appears as part fish. Paradoxically, in the end Eveline shrinks from contact with water. She denies to herself the bliss of liberation which the sea-voyage and the prospect of Buenos Aires seem to offer. But while she negates her fabulous dream-counterpart, this *nix* of legend, she affirms her tense duality in the everyday world; she is female-mother to the family and male-surrogate at the inevitable decline of her father into old age and imminent death. (*Nix* is used also as an exclamation to forbid something; it operates here as a taunting suggestion that Eveline's father is yielding his rule to the feminine principle.) The father's blackthorn stick, a sexual emblem in a class with "broken harmonium," street-organ, and iron railing, represents the repressive force that contradicts the usual generative function of the male.

The notion of change in life creeps into her consciousness as an effect of boredom, induced and heightened by the meditated elopement with Frank. The omnipresent dust of the room, the indifferent and even scornful attitude of people in the stores, "the invariable squabble for money," and so on all set her mind craving for a change in mood and atmosphere, a release into the fantasy-realm of music, theater, and distant exotic landscapes, hinted at by the frank, holiday exuberance of her lover. In the room, conceived as the mold of her intimate self, she has remained an inseparable part of the quiet anonymous past: "And yet during all those years she had never found out the name of the priest whose yellowing photograph hung on the wall above the broken harmonium beside the coloured print of the promises made to Blessed Margaret Mary Alacoque." The "broken harmonium" indicates spiritual sloth and frustrated desire of wholeness; the unknown priest, who represents the general failure of fatherhood (or, as one critic suggests, of Ireland's "disenfranchised God"), is the fugitive and derelict betrayer of the faith.[1] Eveline's "promises made to Blessed Margaret" foreshadow the promise to Frank that she breaks, overcome by sheer animalistic terror.

Eveline's musings at the window (window and gate serve as motifs of escape) summon images of the past, which are immediately judged in terms of her present

---

1. William Bysshe Stein, in "The Effects of Eden in Joyce's 'Eveline,'" *Renascence* 15 (Spring 1963): 124–26, interprets the story as an exploration of Eveline's spiritual "velleity," her self-assertive desires; and an illustration of the effects of Original Sin as manifested in Eveline's lustful egotism, and "the willful rebellion of flesh against the demands of spirit."

affair. Frank's manly, open, chivalric qualities coalesce
into his role as savior: "He was standing at the gate, his
peaked cap pushed back on his head and his hair tumbled
forward over a face of bronze." Idyllic associations crystallize in his figure; his ways of courting her make her
pleasantly confused and elated. His attachment to music
transforms him into a creative, renewing force who will
somehow restore the "broken harmonium" of her life and
assure her a happy, innocent future. Frank's "siren song"
of affection, like the organ-music presiding at her mother's
death (Death seems to be the organ-player equated with
the promise of distant, future ecstasy), initiates Eveline's
recognition of the constricting milieu, and a reversal of
her intention to withdraw from it.

The stream of Eveline's consciousness, at first dragged
down by the inertia of her temperament, seems impelled
by the pleasure-urge until she is jolted back into everyday
actuality by her father's objection. She sympathizes with
her father's plight; in essence she embodies the female,
conserving principle. The sentence in the middle of the
story, "The evening deepened in the avenue," intimates
her attitude of acceptance of, or acquiescence in, the fact
that in serving her parents lies the organic premise for
the knowledge of her true being. Significantly, the two
white letters of farewell "grew indistinct." Her father has
entered a stage of eclipse: "Not long before, when she had
been laid up for a day, he had read her out a ghost story
and made toast for her at the fire." Her once-brutal father
is now subdued and mellowed. While brooding over her
lot, her time "running out" (as time ran out for her
deranged mother), she hears the street organ playing;
and the melancholy air of Italy reinforces her elegiac mood
and setting, reviving the "last night of her mother's illness" and the enigmatic words that punctuated "that life
of commonplace sacrifices closing in final craziness"—

"Derevaun Seraun! Derevaun Seraun!"[2] The father curses
the Italian, but the mother—if the construing of her words
as "the end of pleasure is pain" is correct—ironically belies
the drift of her life: death is her escape from pain. I suggest, however, that the mother's cry represents an anagram
of the prolonged sounds of "drown" and "sea," becoming
thus a mimetic device which anticipates the final catastrophe. It also prefigures the ambivalent nature of Frank's
offer: liberation, for Eveline's mother, signified death.
Eveline is a *persona* of the mother's self, resurrected and
given another chance; what is the probability of her re-
versing her former fate?

The climax of her experience evolves as Frank's mysterious figure is gradually defined. We never apprehend
him directly except as an effect, an impression of transcendence, which he produces in her. The impulse of
terror accompanying her escape from home drives Eveline
not to Frank's arms but to "the swaying crowd in the sta-
tion at the North Wall." The wall and the crowd constitute an enormous barrier, reminding her of her duty,
complicating the "maze of distress" which "awoke a nausea
in her body." The commotion, the disorderly sights and
sounds, dizzy her; she has, in truth, no felt knowledge of
Frank. One distinct image sharpens the internal conflict
between filial devotion and individual will in Eveline:
"Through the wide doors of the sheds she caught a glimpse
of the black mass of the boat, lying in beside the quay
wall, with illumined portholes." Monstrous death, not her
lover-savior, dominates her expectant consciousness. She is

----

2. Professor John V. Kelleher of Harvard, in a letter to me (March 11,
1966), discusses the meaning of the mother's death-cry: "My own feeling
is that 'derevaun seraun' is only the rambling delirium of a dying woman.
But I can't prove that it isn't Irish *as heard by and inaccurately remembered by Eveline* who knows no Irish. Neither can Henchy prove that it
is Irish for 'the end of pleasure is pain.' He would have to account for
the "v" sound which is a corrupt addition if his translation is accurate."
For Henchy's opinion, see William York Tindall, *A Reader's Guide to
James Joyce* (New York: Noonday Press, 1959), p. 22.

overwhelmed by the dissonant, anarchic turmoil of the quay. The convergence of sights and sounds builds into a moment resembling the time she heard her mother's death cry, which had filled her with "a sudden impulse of terror." Her mind plunges into chaos. "The long mournful whistle," then the bell that "clanged upon her heart," force her to recoil; her external action corresponds to internal reaction—a physiological reflex of her psyche. She is going through an experience analogous to her mother's. The shocking novelty of her surroundings destroys her illusions by first distorting her senses: "All the seas of the world rumbled about her heart. He was drawing her into them: he would drown her. She gripped with both hands at the iron railing."

Frank's invitation seems to echo her mother's parting words, generating in her spasms of terror: "She set her white face to him, passive, like a helpless animal. Her eyes gave him no sign of love or farewell or recognition." Frank has known and seduced Eveline; but he did not know that her surrender to uncontrollable instinct would also be the force that will reject him. Eveline's confrontation with her lover excites nausea, less by a guilty recollection of her mother's prophecy than by the abrupt, violent, dislocating force of this impulsive act to deny her larger self and its commitment to parents, home, and the past. Such commitment decides her fate. She risks pain in the pursuit of a pleasure beyond the primitive satisfactions of domestic life—but the pain is convulsive, uncomprehended.

One can theorize that Eveline's predicament illustrates the axiom that "character is fate." On the basis of her susceptible nature, which is restrained on the surface by domestic duties, one can predicate of her situation the inevitable conflict between duty and passion, between fanciful self-indulgence and sober acceptance of daily suffering. Eveline is caught between the desire for "some-

body to protect her" and the compelling urge to fulfill
her sexual role. Her mother's ghost finally wins.

Joyce has skillfully rendered Eveline's character more
vividly in her act of realizing the past than in her impulse
of visualizing the future. Eveline herself is the agent of
permanence, avoiding change when she deflects her attention from the reality around her and fixes her senses on the
need for a secure, stable position. Thus Frank appears not
as savior but as an agent of death about to drown her.
The time-sequence of the narrative adjusts the proportion
of inner past and external present by emphasizing
Eveline's communal-oriented sensibility. We are thus led
to identify with Eveline's lot by being constantly im-
mersed in her sustained introspections, although the fact
that we also know a lot more than she does is responsible
for the effect of irony we discern in the manipulation of
the plot. Joyce's handling of plot and characterization ultimately reconciles the diverging movements in Eveline's
self. Eveline has preserved in herself the instinctive love
of place, with the house and her milieu embodying the
continuity of affections, which, though conservative in
impact, anchor her to the enduring matrix of her inmost
being.

5

AFTER THE RACE

JOYCE'S SUBTLE HANDLING OF SEQUENCE OF EVENTS AND
emotional rhythm distinguishes "After the Race" from the
preceding stories in *Dubliners*. While the image of the
race and the physical motions of the youthful group suggest Jim Doyle's aspiration for status, they also focus on
the eventual outcome of the race. In fact, the title emphasizes clearly the importance of what happens "after
the race." On multiple levels, "race" denotes competition
(*agon*) and highlights disparity in breed (class, national-
ity, pedigree, etc.) , punning also on "after the father" in
analogous manner. All these levels operate in determining
the structural significance of each incident in the story.

Critics have alleged that Joyce, presumably unac-
quainted with the milieu of the upper class, has failed to
portray it with any degree of plausibility or cogent veri-
similitude. But this is a charge that deliberately misreads
the thematic concern of the story, that is, what happens
to Jimmy Doyle—*happens* being used in this context in
the unwittingly receptive sense. For in both the ride and
the gambling scene, it is Jimmy vis-à-vis the foreigners
who engages us: his impressionable mind registers more
than what he is aware of in only a vague, inchoate fashion.

High-pitched adventure and hilarious excitement function
as means of Jimmy's involvement with the external world.
The tone of discovery announced by the last word, "Daybreak!" clinches in a concrete image the argument of the
plot, the action of the story.

Here and throughout *Dubliners,* Joyce is preoccupied
with the problem of defining the limits of illusion and the
province of reality. His method essentially revolves around
the disclosure of character in a situation of sensory vivid-
ness and exactitude. Take the first paragraph, which combines descriptive-narrative material and omniscient author's comment:

> The cars came scudding in towards Dublin, running evenly
> like pellets in the groove of the Naas Road. At the crest of
> the hill at Inchicore sightseers had gathered in clumps to
> watch the cars careering homeward and through this channel
> of poverty and inaction the Continent sped its wealth and
> industry. Now and again the clumps of people raised the
> cheer of the gratefully oppressed. Their sympathy, however,
> was for the blue cars—the cars of their friends, the French.

This passage contains in microcosm the basic analogic pattern of the story. The word *scudding* (*scud*—to move,
run, or fly swiftly) anticipates Farley's yacht, foreground-
ing its nautical reference to "running rapidly before the
wind, especially before a gale with little or no sail set."
The motif of reckless imprudence is also introduced by
the verb's connotation. Jimmy has metaphorically little
or no sail set in his voyage toward the upper rank. In its
general sense, *scud* implies swift movement against strong
resistance: Jimmy's desperate effort to ingratiate himself
in high society, aggravated by his parents' coaxing, is thus
clarified. But the cars are mocked in appearance, described as *pellets;* the "groove of Naas Road," called "this
channel of poverty and inaction" leading to Dublin, re-

flects the satiric scorn of the author at the abject "clump" of spectators. In their passive role the Irish behold the marvelous "blue cars" of the French; this crowd of the "gratefully oppressed"—an ironic phrase that aptly fits Jimmy—cheers only at the "virtual" victors, for the real winner is a German car.

Like the chosen self-deception of the cheering rabble, Jimmy's response to Riviere and the bustling life with which he is associated is ambiguous and uncritical. Notice that Jimmy is "too excited to be genuinely happy." His career, motivated by the hypocritical desires of his father who is "alluded to in the Dublin newspapers as a merchant prince," culminates in a pitiful disaster of physical (monetary) and spiritual loss. Set against "successful Gallicism," the Doyles become sad victims of the experts in games and sportive masquerades. We find that the bright commercial future of Segouin and Riviere has been insured by the "advance" orders offered by Jimmy's father, undercutting the eulogistic reputation as "advanced Nationalist." The play on *advance*, like the pejorative insinuation of "voluntaries" in the gambling scene, betrays the foolish and vain expectations of this Irish *nouveau riche*. Jimmy's pride in mixing with wealthy people in a luxurious car heightens his lack of pride in his own self, in his own integrity.

Jimmy's father, a lucky butcher who made good, determines the fate of the son, described as "twenty-six years of age" with "rather innocent-looking grey eyes." Jimmy's adolescence has been unnaturally prolonged, for the father still governs: "His father, remonstrative, but covertly proud of the excess, had paid his bills and brought him home." This ambivalence infects the whole household, with their inner doubts and hesitancies, their blindness to actuality, their readiness to be gulled:

In Jimmy's house this dinner had been pronounced an

occasion. A certain pride mingled with his parents' trepidation, a certain eagerness, also, to play fast and loose for the
names of great foreign cities have at least this virtue. Jimmy,
too, looked very well when he was dressed and, as he stood
in the hall giving a last equation to the bows of his dress tie,
his father may have felt even commercially satisfied at having
secured for his son qualities often unpurchaseable. His father,
therefore, was unusually friendly with Villona and his manner expressed a real respect for foreign accomplishments;
but this subtlety of his host was probably lost upon the
Hungarian, who was beginning to have a sharp desire for
his dinner.

Pride and trepidation characterize the parents' reaction to
Jimmy's initiation into reputable society. But poor Jimmy,
given his elegant dress, cannot sustain that last "equation" of himself with an illusion. Although the father
as host might have sincere feelings of appreciation for
culture and urban finesse, this gesture is lost upon Villona,
a curious blend of delicate *artiste* and brute.

Villona appears as the heroic figure who can reconcile
mechanics and music, instinctive aplomb and refined taste.
Gifted with charm and reserve, he manifests the relaxing
buoyance required for adjusting to actuality. Physical enjoyment appeals to his "optimistic" nature; he has control
of himself enough to refrain from being duped, and to
take the proceedings with tongue-in-cheek indifference.
While Jimmy suffers exhaustion in pursuit of excitement,
Villona's "purposeless" exercise of his skill translates mo-
toring into delightful vibrations of music. His conduct,
simpler and less demanding, displays a conviction and confidence lacking in Jimmy's artificially induced mood. Villona represents the spontaneous activity of the will as he
is perceived singing "voluntaries" for the engrossed
players; he serves as the bearer of tidings when he, flinging
open the cabin door and standing silhouetted in grey daylight, utters the ominous yet somehow liberating recogni-

tion: "Daybreak, gentlemen!" That climax, the culmina-
tion of the exclamatory character and boisterous pace of
the last episode, comes with the arrival of dawn and the
game's end. It is also the "finish" of Jimmy's race for
distinction.

This aura of distinction which Jimmy attaches to the
French youth is entailed by the racial nature of the Irish
(see the first paragraph) and its effect on a vulnerable
temperament of extreme susceptibility. Jimmy's companions, a merry "cargo of hilarious youth," are charming,
are shallow but entertaining (Villona, though poor, is a
brilliant pianist). Jimmy's frantic ambition carries with
it its objective correspondence in the race: "Rapid motion through space elates one; so does notoriety; so does
the possession of money." His enthusiasm, the frothy by-
product of indiscriminate commitments, eventually betrays him.

Jimmy's case is efficiently defined by Joyce in a few
particularizing strokes. His clumsy grappling for the
Frenchman's good will leads to awkward, painful confusion: "The Frenchmen flung their laughter and light
words over their shoulders and often Jimmy had to strain
forward to catch the quick phrase. This was not altogether
pleasant for him, as he had nearly always to make a deft
guess at the meaning and shout back a suitable answer in
the face of a high wind. Besides Villona's humming
would confuse anybody; the noise of the car, too." Music
and machine contribute to Jimmy's frustration; the rapid
motor car and the opposing wind drown all communication between Jimmy and what he considers his "superiors." Strangely, Jimmy seems unable to salvage his dis-
integrating self despite his flickering knowledge that there
is something amiss in all his dealings with the foreigners:
"At the control Segouin had presented him to one of the
French competitors and, in answer to his confused murmur of compliment, the swarthy face of the driver had

disclosed a line of shining white teeth. It was pleasant
after that honour to return to the profane world of spectators amid nudges and significant looks."

With the breakdown in communication, Jimmy perceives "the swarthy face" disclosing "shiny white teeth"—
intimations of fraudulence. Jimmy, like Villona, is more
at home in the naïve, elemental world of gestures and
wordless intimacy. As an "inheritor of solid instincts," he
could understand the serious implication of staking his
fortune in a risky enterprise. He could practise prudence,
confine himself "within the limits of reasonable reckless-
ness." Yet his sensibility proves his own undoing. Although he has the imaginative capacity to foresee and
rationalize, his mode of response toward wealth is chiefly
a willing submission to its power of release, its indulgence
of the senses and the irrational: "Jimmy set out to trans-
late into days' work that lordly car in which he sat. How
smoothly it ran. In what style they had come careering
along the country roads! The journey laid a magical finger
on the genuine pulse of life and gallantly the machinery
of human nerves strove to answer the bounding course
of the blue swift animal." "The machinery of human
nerves" behaves with fairly definite and predictable consequences, open as it is to manipulation from external
factors and influences.

The motor car and its elating speed is one of the major
factors that convey Jimmy to his catastrophe, his loss of
money and investment. The people near the Bank in
Dame Street paid homage "to the snorting motor," as if
it were a fabulous monster to be propitiated. (Note the
equivalence of machine and machine-like organism in
Joyce's phrase "the machinery of human nerves.") The
car's maleficent role fades off in the foggy, shifting atmosphere of urban flux: "They walked northward with a
curious feeling of disappointment in the exercise, while
the city hung its pale globes of light above them in a haze

of summer evening. . . . That night the city wore the
mask of a capital. The five young men strolled along
Stephen's Green in a faint cloud of aromatic smoke." A
gradual de-realization of environment by a technique of
impressionism and optic stylization may be observed in
Joyce's descriptions: "They drove by the crowd, blended
now into soft colours, to a music of merry bells. . . . It
was a serene summer night; the harbour lay like a darkened mirror at their feet." The setting assumes the coloring of fantasy and forecasts the "dark stupor" to which
Jimmy succumbs in the end, after absorbing the tumult
of impressions in his waking hours.

There is never really any sign of conflict between Jimmy
and the foreigners, because Jimmy has offered his impressionable self to be the complete prey of appearances.
Segouin and Routh have led all the way, Segouin as tactful
manipulator of the conversation and "shepherd" of the
company and Routh as the victor who "routs" his oppo-
nents. Segouin operates the car, the beetle-like machine
that serves as the vehicle of Jimmy's fate. Jimmy's generous openness to the world obscures his clear perception
of facts: "Jimmy, whose imagination was kindling, conceived the lively youth of the Frenchmen twined elegantly
upon the firm framework of the Englishman's manner."
Villona mesmerizes him with musical know-how, while
Riviere ingeniously dazzles him with candid fluency on
"the triumph of French mechanicians." To the shrewd
and experienced Continentals, the ingenuous Farley and
the naïve Jimmy become victims. Both are seduced by the
smooth polish of the Frenchmen (Riviere dances to the
waltz as a lady) .

In the yacht, the vessel which symbolizes the starting-
point of the voyage into the dangerous sea of life, Jimmy
acquiesces in his fall as a result of self-generated fatality.
He is distracted and beguiled by the flashing revelry, the
ceremony "for form's sake": "What merriment! Jimmy

took his part with a will; this was seeing life, at least." The
depreciative qualification "at least" modulates Jimmy's
participation into a developing notion of degrees of knowledge. Formality of manners degenerates into burlesque;
and Jimmy, impotent to defy the waves of excitement and
the undertow of habitual delusion, sells his identity to
the demon of chance. Adventure and heady steering of
consciousness pervade the rhythm of the last "race":

> Cards! Cards! The table was cleared. Villona returned
> quietly to his piano and played voluntaries for them. The
> other men played game after game, flinging themselves boldly
> into the adventure. They drank the health of the Queen of
> Hearts and of the Queen of Diamonds. Jimmy felt ob-
> scurely the lack of an audience: the wit was flashing. Play
> ran very high and paper began to pass. Jimmy did not know
> exactly who was winning but he knew that he was losing.
> But it was his own fault for he frequently mistook his cards
> and the other men had to calculate his I.O.U.'s for him.
> They were devils of fellows but he wished they would stop:
> it was getting late. Someone gave the toast of the yacht *The
> Belle of Newport* and then someone proposed one great game
> for a finish.

Life, symbolized by the vessel, is exalted here in its
terrible glory and heedless destructiveness. Caught in a
situation where the sophisticated gamblers prove treacherous and the unworldly Jimmy Doyle the loser, Jimmy
proves too immature to "embark" on the perilous voyage
of life. Ultimately, his fate "transpires," with the convergence of innate disposition and circumstance. In this
drama of situations, the central protagonist turns out to
be a pathetic victim.

Jimmy's whole experience, which draws him ultimately
to a realization of his folly, takes on the analogy of a race,
a gamble, or a game, just as his father's fortune was
amassed under the patronage of Lady Fortune. But the

dark stupor of his exulting self, instead of concealing truth, gives way to the piercing illumination of day (with its gloomy, warning "shaft of grey light") and the moment of discovery. Jimmy loses the race when fate, truth, overtakes him; his name (suggesting a burglar's crowbar used to pry open a vault or case) underlines his function as a means or tool acted upon so as to disclose what is concealed: the total situation of the character himself. Intoxicating music and dizzying dance effect a distancing of reality and convert the catastrophic game into some crazy, kaleidoscopic event which, upon dissolving, forces Jimmy to confront life with a sharpened faculty for defining what is momentary and what is permanent, what is false and what is genuine. Joyce's vision of life as a conflict between mask and flesh, sordid fact and cloudy ideals, is dramatized here as the ordeal of personality through experience until it achieves, "after the race," its own saving confession of guilt and acceptance of responsibility.

6

TWO GALLANTS

AFTER "IVY DAY IN THE COMMITTEE ROOM" THIS STORY
pleased Joyce most. Arguing with his censor-haunted pub-
lisher, he declared that he would willingly sacrifice five
of the other stories if by so doing he could preserve this
story in the volume.[1] We can perhaps explain Joyce's
pleasure in this story not only as an effective satire against
his countrymen's degradation, or an elegiac hymn to Ireland's bondage, but also as a formal aesthetic whole with
distinct parts so proportioned and disposed as to achieve
the specific emotional effect sought by the artist. That
effect, and the invention of the means to produce it, surely
provide the reason for the profound pleasure Joyce felt
in the story. It is a pleasure inherent in the act of conceiv-
ing and executing the action of a narrative which redeems
the despicable characters depicted in it by locating the
internal necessity of their life in the cosmos of art.

To define the internal necessity of this work, we might
begin by reconstructing what Joyce's problems were in
composing the narrative structure. It is obvious that the
action or object represented in the plot centers on Lenehan. But although this protagonist focalizes the incidents

---

1. *Letters*, vol. 1, p. 62.

of the plot, what informs these incidents and their arrangement is the nature of the change the sequence is made to effect in the protagonist. This change occurs in the thought of the main character, reiterating a habitual mechanism of his personality, without materially altering his fortune or his character as an ethical human being. The change he undergoes is not simple but complex, not static but dynamic, for the plot shows the protagonist passing through a succession of two or more states in three episodes that constitute the action of the story.

In analyzing the kind of change the protagonist experiences, we must concentrate on the middle part of the story, where Lenehan is shown alone, shifting for himself, while Corley proceeds to experiment with his girl. Lenehan's appearance suggests a distinct change: "Now that he was alone his face looked older. A swift upsurge of discontent possessed him. He found trivial all that was meant to charm him and did not answer the glances which invited him to be bold." Morose and somber, his mood radically contrasts with his gay, convulsed body as it responds to Corley's monologue in the opening paragraphs. His animated, vicarious enjoyment of Corley's sexual escapades also characterizes Lenehan's appearance as a "sporting vagrant." Removed from the presence of others, he feels boredom encroaching—until the partaking of cheap food in the *Refreshment Bar* puts his mind to work and produces a complete turnabout in his thoughts.

Before that inevitable and yet sudden movement toward self-disclosure, Joyce establishes in the first episode the range and scope of probabilities operating in the character of Lenehan. When we first meet the two young men, we develop certain expectations about what they are going to do next, what their thoughts and feelings will be. Joyce's technique of characterization is never an end in itself, only a means to the dramatic externalization of the powers that make up the *ethos* of a protagonist. Static features

participate with acts and utterances to convey the essence
of personality. Take Lenehan's figure. Although he is
almost pushed off the path by his companion's "rudeness,"
he still displays "an amused listening face." Later we are
informed that "he was insensitive to all kinds of dis-
courtesy." Lenehan treads the margin of the beaten path,
yielding to Corley's advance. Lenehan's wheezing laughter,
the constant waves of expression that his friend's talk stirs
in his face, his convulsed body, his eyes "twinkling with
cunning enjoyment"—all these define the powerful hold
exerted on his impulsive and susceptible nature by Corley.

While Lenehan's appearance—his yachting cap, his
waterproof jauntily slung in toreador fashion, his breeches
and white rubber shoes—expresses youth and indicates
the positive, hopeful side of his character, the other half
suggests negative and discouraging possibilities: rotund
waist, scant and gray hair, "his face, when the waves of
expression had passed over it, had a ravaged look." Symp-
tomatic of the capacity for despair and delight shown most
clearly in the concluding episode, these two aspects of
Lenehan's character anticipate his inner crisis in the
Refreshment Bar (the name hints ambivalently of both
renewal and relapse) .

Our expectations of Lenehan dressed as a vigorous
young gallant, a genteel voyager of the streets, are sharply
discounted by his equivocal physiognomy. Not wholly
fawning or servile, he seems at first erratic and evasive.
But Joyce soon frames his behavior in the opening scene
with a résumé of his past, isolating the typical or ascendant
qualities of nimble tact and discreet knowingness. When
Lenehan becomes serious and silent after his jesting refrain, the narrative shifts to a portrait of his public image.
The trait of flexibility at the edge of gatherings—note his
manner of keeping up with Corley—is given by the statement: "He had a brave manner of coming up at a party
of them in a bar and of holding himself nimbly at the

borders of the company until he was included in a round."
Reputed a "leech," his adroitness and eloquence had prevented "a general policy against him" from materializing.
Even his means of livelihood puzzled his friends, though
in Joyce's felicitous idiom we detect a hidden note of
admiration: "No one knew how he achieved the stern
task of living. . . ."
    From this background supplement to Lenehan's drama-
tized behavior, we are furnished the element of the
unconditional in his psyche. Lenehan's adroitness, balanced by his leech-like parasitism, explains his treatment
of sexual affairs as games, the bet with Corley, his circular
perambulation, and his dependence on Corley for emotional gratification. The poor, romantic Lenehan preys
on Corley just as the arrogant Corley preys on his easy
women.
    The subject of Corley's monologue clears up when
Lenehan's query "And where did you pick her up . . . ?"
introduces us to the obsessive concern of his friend. Corley's language as he brags about his sponging on tarts
reveals him as a conscienceless gigolo and a shameless
parasite. The tributes he receives ("two bloody fine
cigars," etc.) foreshadow the small gold coin he wheedles
from the girl. With his bloated ego and crude, sensual
nature, Corley emerges as the real leech. He indulges in
the privilege of being base by procuring money from
easily deceived servant girls. Corley's libertinism projects
a deceptively "gallant" image that encourages him to
pretend that he is "a bit of class," yet in truth he proves
"hairy" and swaggeringly heartless.
    After giving us a sufficiently revealing example of
Corley's thoughts and sentiments, Joyce then proceeds to
delineate his physical appearance, with emphasis on the
perpetually sweating "globular and oily head." His stiff
frame and gait indicative of his father's calling as police
inspector, added to his rapacious self-indulgence, makes

him the incarnation of abusive power: "He knew the
inner side of all affairs and was fond of delivering final
judgment."

To accuse Lenehan of being a willing accomplice of
Corley's bloodsucking would be to ignore signs of his
inner misgivings, if not distaste, at his friend's ways. Consider how his "cunning enjoyment" alternates with the
ravaged look of his face, how he laughs noiselessly, his
voice "winnowed of vigour" becoming "serious and silent." Notice also the supposition he makes about what
the fine tart Corley picked up would expect ("Maybe she
thinks you'll marry her . . ."). His noiseless laughing and
his emphatic compliment to Corley's morally obnoxious
experience seem to stir up inner promptings in his mind:
"Corley smiled at the passing girls but Lenehan's gaze
was fixed on the large faint moon circled with a double
halo. He watched earnestly the passing of the grey web
of twilight across its face." Doubtful of his friend's luck
in constantly exploiting women, Lenehan is assured by
Corley that he will make fair game of his prey. The
ironic overtone of Lenehan's praise and blunt narrative
commentary engages our interest, if not sympathy, for
Lenehan and his efforts at gallantry:

—You're what I call a gay Lothario, said Lenehan. And the
proper bit of a Lothario, too!
A shade of mockery relieved the servility of his manner.
To save himself he had the habit of leaving his flattery
open to the interpretation of raillery. But Corley had not
a subtle mind.

Lenehan's capacity for subtle mockery suggests an inner
life that will complicate his future conduct with Corley,
whom he accuses, in a half-jesting but tragic way, of being
a "base betrayer!"—for converting an honest girl into a
prostitute.

The remaining conversation between them before they sight Corley's girl confirms our early suspicion that Lenehan's tactful intelligence does not wholly coincide with Corley's brutal licentiousness, although, because of his leech-like attachment to his friend, Lenehan cannot, without being inconsistent, rebuke him. When, for example, Lenehan says that he wants to take a look at the girl, Corley gives an unpleasant grin and accuses his friend: "Are you trying to get inside me?"—a proof of his suspicious and deceitful nature.

Before the two mock-gallants separate, they agree on their meeting-place, with Corley's brusque indifference demarcating him from Lenehan's solicitous posture. Lenehan's scrutiny of Corley's victim serves to emphasize certain affinities between her peculiar appearance and Lenehan's. The discrepancy between Lenehan's garment and his real feelings parallels the girl's attractive dress and her grotesque face: broad nostrils, "straggling mouth which lay open in a contented leer," and two projecting front teeth. Some interpreters even conceive of her as a vampire, on the evidence of her umbrella, inverted flowers, predatory look, and so on. A close kinship exists between the girl and Lenehan: he sports a yachting cap, the girl a white sailor hat. Lenehan is squat and ruddy, the girl has a "stout short muscular body." Both carry shield-like devices: waterproof, umbrella.

Finally, we reach the point from which we began: the crucial incident where a change in thought overtakes Lenehan. One signal preparation for this change is Lenehan's behavior in strumming the railings of Duke's lawn with his finger, his movements controlled by the harpist's melody he has heard on the way to Corley's tryst. His susceptibility to external sensuous appeal reveals an emotional nature given to fantasy, capable of indulging in the simple delight of satisfying his hunger or consoling himself with beguiling daydreams. Skillful in inventing amuse-

ment for others, Lenehan now pursues his wild visions
in a desperate effort to fill up the hollow duration of
existence. The sordid restaurant he patronizes and the
cheap food he enjoys demonstrate his unspoiled instinctive
self, at the same time heightening the incongruity of his
hopes for a bourgeois marriage to compensate for the
magnitude of his poverty. But the curve downward and
upward of his spirit betrays a hidden capacity for self-
knowledge:

> In his imagination he beheld the pair of lovers walking
> along some dark road; he heard Corley's voice in deep ener-
> getic gallantries and saw again the leer of the young woman's
> mouth. This vision made him feel keenly his own poverty
> of purse and spirit. He was tired of knocking about, of pull-
> ing the devil by the tail, of shifts and intrigues. He would be
> thirty-one in November. Would he never get a good job?
> Would he never have a home of his own? He thought how
> pleasant it would be to have a warm fire to sit by and a good
> dinner to sit down to. He had walked the streets long
> enough with friends and with girls. He knew what those
> friends were worth: he knew the girls too. Experience had
> embittered his heart against the world. But all hope had not
> left him. He felt better after having eaten than he had felt
> before, less weary of his life, less vanquished in spirit. He
> might yet be able to settle down in some snug corner and
> live happily if he could only come across some good simple-
> minded girl with a little of the ready.

Experience has embittered Lenehan's heart against the
world, but his unease seems caused more by hunger and
solitude than by the habit of introspective examination of
conscience. He habitually exists on the surface of life.

Lenehan's virtue of fidelity to his word makes him the
antithesis of the treacherous, cynical Corley. Yet, because
Lenehan has no real individuality, requisite for being
self-sufficient, he fails to realize his defect and to achieve

integrity by fulfilling the claim of the truths he apprehends when meditating alone in the *Refreshment Bar*. Afflicted with the malady of projecting his own needs as someone else's, Lenehan suffers "all the pangs and thrills of his friend's situation as well as those of his own." Having been drawn into Lenehan's imagination, we now eagerly anticipate with him the outcome of Corley's adventure.

So far, we have seen how character develops in conformity with the demands of the action which the plot actualizes. Whatever symbolic meanings or thematic levels of value can be plumbed here, may be seen to radiate from the network of expectations that are fulfilled or foiled. Obscure and pointless at first glance, the bare factual happenings—the reported elliptical dialogue, the realistic notations of setting, and the like—exhibit a progression in the nexus between cause and effect: the immediate occasion links up with the past, which adds consistency to the logic of behavior until the pattern of the plot reaches a stage of reversal. This change, though occurring in Lenehan's mind, suffices to contribute a counteracting element that makes the end both predictable and wonderful.

Corley initiates the movement of the plot toward the end: his story about his encounter with "a fine tart," his success, and the hinted peril of being compromised prods Lenehan to doubt whether his huckster friend will "pull it off all right" this time. This mysterious task is none other than the extortion of money from a "slavey." The interval from the separation to their reunion shows us the change in mood and attitude that temporarily threatens to disrupt the bond between the two friends. Lenehan's nature, however, and the argument he entertains against Corley's success, make the end somewhat unexpected.

In each of the incidents that constitute the plot, we

perceive a vertical continuity tying up by recurrent imagery, allusions, and diction all the events that retard the
forward movement or advance it by multiplying possible
solutions to problems arising in the interaction between
characters. The exposition of the friendship between Lenehan and Corley implies either a total breakaway by
Lenehan, or a renewed identification with his friend. The
countermovement to the maintenance of Lenehan's outer
subservience to Corley, extending to the possibilities of
his capacity for detachment and mockery, erupts when
Lenehan begins to reflect on his life in the *Refreshment
Bar*. But his inner anguish fails to permanently modify
the core of Lenehan's self. Because of ingrained habits,
he misses the chance to reform himself or alter his judgment of his surroundings. The inner tension resolves itself
when, given his clever inventiveness, he diverts his galling
despair to a return to his shiftless wandering, his idle
and wasteful drifting.

Thus, when we confront the two men at their reunion,
we receive enlightenment as we view Corley's opened palm,
a grave gesture that at once denies, and absolves his
"disciple" of, guilt. Enacting a solemn ritual of revealing
a secret, Corley delivers an ironic thrust: a receiver of coin,
he has surrendered his integrity once more. This token
payment of Corley's lustful service, lighting up his mean
and dismal existence, signifies the moral advantage of his
victim (contrast the stable house of the girl as vantage
point with the gallants' drifting condition). Lenehan's
early exclamation "Base betrayer," masking bitter envy,
turns out to be the appropriate charge delivered by a man
whose hopeful illusion about Corley's girl (that she will
escape from Corley's clutches) is betrayed.

Joyce's craftsmanship enables the ending to produce the
precise revelation needed to purge Lenehan of anxiety and
miserable bafflement without foregoing the chance to
manipulate our responses in condemning Corley as a

shameless male prostitute. Corley's gesture arrests us because it effects not only a denial of sympathy connatural
to man but also a sell-out of his friend's hope and trust—
that the girl will frustrate his friend's design.

Lenehan's self-justification during his solitary musings
in the restaurant provides the impulse that calls for Corley's failure—a betrayal of his friend. A frustrated dreamer
himself, Lenehan idealizes the female sex enough for him
to flatter Corley outwardly and despise him inwardly for
his past conquests. Lenehan's nature curiously holds both
realistic and idealistic capacities. In his marginal existence
and poignant estrangement from the organic and communal center of life, Lenehan confronts his rootlessness
and poverty, his absurd vagrancy, with shallow and ineffectual optimism. A shrewd player in a "mug's game,"
he qualifies his sycophantic absorption in Corley's life
with a wonder that, after the spiritual revelation about
his true self, evolves into identification. Corley seems to
embody the unrealized half of Lenehan's psyche. This
may argue for the vital buried force manifested by his
gift of being able to amuse others. Lenehan's life is
flawed by a "negative capability" in his character which
undermines moral commitment of any kind. In Lenehan
are mirrored the conflicting forces of a self-renouncing
imagination and selfish instinctive needs (hunger compels
him to review his personal fate), which precipitate a
change in thought. However, this glimpse of the truth
about himself yields to the more dominant force of the
mask or *persona*, the jesting sentimental leech.

Dealing essentially with a grim vaudeville situation
where a sober satyr and a sophisticated clown play a game
of finding each other out, "Two Gallants" also strikes
the reader as a counterfeit romance with an inverted quest
blaspheming all the norms in the *Book of the Courtier*.
The burlesque pair perform the antics of the game, revealing the gallantry of predatory intriguers in images

of exploitation and lust. Lenehan and Corley are portrayed with fine seriousness and insight that offset any
sign of the narrator's anger or bias. Joyce's sympathetic
dissection of Lenehan's moral deficiency substitutes for
a malicious ferocity a sly sense of humor conveyed in a
sensitive, tactful style that lets the reader draw the inferences supporting an impartial judgment.

Joyce blends lyrical description with a rigorously dis-
criminated presentation of the painful and sordid, pene-
trating realism with feelings-filled imagery, to produce
a witty and parodic diminution of the false sublime and
a critique of sham appearance. In the first paragraph of
the story, Joyce combines melancholy wistfulness with a
touch of decadence: lamps resemble "illumined pearls."
The sentimental aura of autumn fuses with the raw flux
of experience. The contours of things seem blurred, inchoate, with the changing texture of life sending up "into
the warm grey evening air an unchanging unceasing
murmur." Juxtaposed with the "gallantry" of Lenehan
and Corley, the dialectic of permanence and change, of
reality and mimicry, operates with the burden of a sear-
ing irony in the situations presented by the story. Lenehan's alteration in thought remains submerged but subtly
affects his ultimate attitude toward Corley's success.

We comprehend the function of setting as the technique
of representing the characters within the larger context
of the action. The somber gray evening drawn in the
exposition and the "memory of summer" borne on the
circulating air suggest loss and meaningless duration.
Contrasts abound in the sensations evoked by the varied
items in the description: "The streets, shuttered for the
repose of Sunday, swarmed with a gaily coloured crowd."
But such imagery as the interplay of light and dark, of
motion and stillness, simply contributes to the magnitude
of the parts of the representation, parts which cohere

within the complex unity of the action. While representational devices for magnifying or contracting incidents affect the verbal style and thicken the texture, these devices in turn are governed by the organizing principle of the action arranged to effect a specific change in the thought of the protagonist and arouse the required emotional response from us. Consequently, if we seek to discover why the story affects us in the manner it does, we have to examine the way the parts are synthesized in order to promote the ultimate ends of the artist, who is primarily concerned with constructing formal wholes.

From this approach, the central image of the harp that most commentators consider as the key to the meaning Joyce intended in this story, will be seen to be a subordinate though significant part of the mode of representation. We must inquire, then, what function the description of the harp and harpist performs to advance the plot.

The spectacle of the harpist is framed between the first long dialogue, where Corley sums up his reminiscence with "She's a fine decent tart," and the sight of Corley's prospective "victim." While the mournful music of "Silent O Moyle" expands the patriotic theme of Ireland's rebellious and immortal spirit, and the harp, conceived as feminine ("weary alike of the eyes of strangers and of her master's hands"), may be said to represent Ireland's fate, it seems necessary to point out that the spectacle serves first of all the function of an apt comment on Corley's handling of women (note the harpist's heedless, weary manner) and a preparation for the tart's appearance. One may consider the allusions in Tom Moore's gentle air as formal devices to unify various implications in the conduct of the characters, giving to their motives a universal extension. But the clearest and not the least significant value of the harpist lies in what he contributes to our understanding of Lenehan's character and the change of thought that occurs in him:

> Now that he was alone his face looked older. His gaiety
> seemed to forsake him and, as he came by the railings of the
> Duke's Lawn, he allowed his hand to run along them. The
> air which the harpist had played began to control his move-
> ments. His softly padded feet played the melody while his
> fingers swept a scale of variations idly along the railings
> after each group of notes.

Lenehan's kinship with the harpist assigns him a role of
heedless, weary caretaker of feminine honor that would
force him to oppose Corley. On the other hand, what
Joyce foregrounds here is Lenehan's sensitive and responsible inner self which, released from the constraints
of his diffused ego, possesses a wholeness that saves him
from absolute depravity. Lenehan secretly desires Corley's
failure: "An intimation of the result pierced him like the
point of a sharp instrument. He knew Corley would
fail. . . ." Baffled and menaced, he makes the most shatter-
ing discovery: he has moved to the very opposite of
Corley's position. The nature of the change in Lenehan's
thought thus contradicts the alleged circularity of his
efforts. The moon's double halo, refracting vision, fore-
bodes Lenehan's eclipsed feelings toward Corley. In the
Refreshment Bar, Lenehan's emotions are "refracted" into
desperate bitterness, succeeded by superficial hopefulness.
Corley's adventure—its exciting and its depraved sides—
accounts for Lenehan's ambivalent feeling of frantic
dejection and impulsive fear in the concluding scene.

7

THE BOARDING HOUSE

FIVE PARAGRAPHS OF TELLING DESCRIPTION AND SUMMARY, the conventional exposition, make up the beginning and offer the premises for the action of "The Boarding House." From this observation it would be easy to conclude that this is, as the handbooks categorize it, a "character story." It is clear that character dominates and moves the sequence of incidents that constitute the plot. But on further analysis one will perceive that the characters here are significant only insofar as they play active or passive roles in advancing or retarding the action of the narrative. Thus the story may be said to exhibit a plot of character.

On the surface, what happens may be construed as a function of Mrs. Mooney's character: Polly and Doran—even Jack and Mr. Mooney—are best understood as figures being acted upon by other stronger forces. But as the narration presents Mrs. Mooney's background, we apprehend certain actions from which we infer ethical import or moral value; these actions arouse such feelings or attitudes as are entailed by the opinions we have of those values. From our knowledge of Mrs. Mooney's actions and their implications, we discern with amazing clarity how the story is all of a piece: a unified, tightly-knit

101

system of events contituting the form of the action in the story.

The plot, then, is a plot of character: the sequence of actions, conceived and moved by Mrs. Mooney's judgment and authoritative voice, springs from her presence. Within this plot a reversal occurs; her fortune is changed in an oblique manner: Polly is vindicated, and Mrs. Mooney's betrayed status is redeemed. Discovery resides in Mr. Doran's recognition that, among the causes of his behavior, passion and instinct prove compelling. Our knowledge of the development of events invites the experience of epiphany, the clarity and integrity of the whole narrative form being insured by the consonance of the parts—incident, character, thought—in fulfilling a thematic purpose.

In trying to illumine the mode in which Mrs. Mooney's character is rendered, one must always conceive of her character as a source of certain effects—that is, as an agent by whose conduct and attitudes such incidents as succeed in due course are made probable. The condition of necessity already governs Mrs. Mooney's past as outlined in the first five paragraphs. But what she will do and what others will do as a result of her decisions will accordingly manifest the quality of being likely or probable as a general consequence of her past. The past reveals itself as a nexus of acts and responses, decisions and motions, whose power to affect others is demonstrated in the dramatized scenes, unified by a single definite place and a temporal continuum, alternating with description and summary.

"Mrs. Mooney was a butcher's daughter." This classic beginning cannot be improved upon as a compact statement of social identity, economical in factual content and graceful in the simplicity of its revelation. Doubly wronged, twice a victim, Mrs. Mooney has no soft spot: far from wistfully "mooning" about the cruel twists in her affairs, she lucidly faces her troubles. Indeed, she forces the issue when she contrives Doran's surrender to her designs. She proves the worth of her origin: "She was a woman who was quite able to keep things to herself: a determined woman. She had married her father's foreman and opened a butcher's shop near Spring Gardens." But this Maytime season of her life, the brief idyllic episode—note the juxtaposition of shop and Spring Gardens, practical experience and natural innocence—ends when her father dies; Mr. Mooney somehow "began to go to the devil."

Joyce thus sets the standard for our evaluation of Mrs. Mooney's actions with the establishment of sympathetic distance: she embodies her father's will in her determination to survive, to triumph despite the strict impositions of a world ruled by men. Her husband, representing the negative masculine principle here, breaks pledges and ruins her business; separation ensues. A surrogate for male guardian and protector, Mrs. Mooney sets up a boardinghouse in which she establishes a semblance of matriarchy; she decrees the laws of totem and taboo. Consonant with her inherited disposition (her father's calling is a token of her firmness), Mrs. Mooney as "The Madam" fixes the measure of value in the house.

Knowing the hard knocks, she hardens; inner pressure makes her as hard as the butcher's cutting-board. But she is a good provider, sociable and warm, her boarders sharing in the atmosphere of domesticity, discussing "with one another the chances of favourites and outsiders." Approximating an archetypal mother figure, she easily assumes the position of household authority. Her "vestal maid," Polly, serves as an extension of her psyche. Not all the dealings in the place, however, are aboveboard—so to speak, for Mrs. Mooney, purposeful and secretive, moves underground, knowing all the follies of the old Adam.

Mrs. Mooney, practically widowed, must prove her birthright. She affirms her independence by a summary

treatment of her husband: "She went to the priest and
got a separation from him with care of the children. She
would give him neither money nor food nor house-room."
Estranged and adrift, the poor husband enlists as "sheriff's
man," a "disreputable" visitor to her daughter, then em-
ployed by a corn-factor. Mrs. Mooney in effect seals him
off from the family by withdrawing her daughter from the
outside world and imprisoning her in the house. Knowing
her own mind, she does not need help from her pitiful
husband. But, wronged and aggrieved, could she ever
forget his threatening her with a cleaver?

Shrewd and quietly calculating, "she dealt with moral
problems as a cleaver deals with meat." Experienced in
her trade, alert and assured, business-minded, calmly determined—these traits definitely transform her into a
stereotype of "The Madam." Her husband dissipates his
energy, whereas she concentrates hers for the deadly, delicate blow of triumph. She executes this stroke in defense
of her daughter's honor, her ostensible object. The father's
ghost incarnates itself in the daughter as Mrs. Mooney
seeks revenge against the male; wronged wife evolves into
outraged mother.

Mrs. Mooney's vindication occurs first in her own mind.
The boardinghouse came into existence because the husband betrayed her trust; now one of the boarders would
reinstate this loss, not as retribution, but as affirmation of
the primal vow in marriage. Doran is chosen as sacrificial
victim. Joyce carefully indicates Mrs. Mooney's strategy
leading to success, the result implied by her command
of the passage of time, her self-confidence, her instinctive
grasp of the entire situation—the resolution of her predicament:

> Mrs. Mooney glanced instinctively at the little gilt clock
> on the mantelpiece as soon as she had become aware through
> her revery that the bell of George's church had stopped ring-

ing. It was seventeen minutes past eleven; she would have lots of time to have the matter out with Mr. Doran and then catch short twelve at Marlborough Street.

This settlement of her daughter's fate is shown as part of Mrs. Mooney's habitual course of action, her daily routine. She will be equal to this challenge as she has been equal to her other functions. She is calculating and meticulous in the handling of her resources, including time. There is a candid picture of her thrifty management —crusts are salvaged for the Tuesday pudding, and her mechanical efficiency follows habit and avoids variety. Her frugality makes her charge for beer and keep "sugar and butter safe under lock and key."

We feel that she wants to salvage her broken marriage by the strict imposition of routine and a code of manners, which accords with her masterful presence as she supervises the maid or the ritual of eating in the establishment; she affirms life itself. As "The Madam," proprietress of the establishment, she fits the tag given to her in the two senses of being a maternal power and "manager" of a lively, attractive daughter. But she has a disciplined pride that offsets the malicious joke connoted by that title.

Mrs. Mooney's frugality intimates that she would conduct things logically, pruning any loose alternative or unprofitable risk. And Joyce's rhetoric, a style of dialectical turns and balances, conveys it effectively: "She had allowed him to live beneath her roof, assuming that he was a man of honour, and he had simply abused her hospitality. He was thirty-four or thirty-five years of age, so that youth could not be pleaded as his excuse; nor could ignorance be his excuse since he was a man who had seen something of the world. He had simply taken advantage of Polly's youth and inexperience: that was evident. The question was: What reparation would he make?"

The enactment of what is bound to happen spins spon-

taneously in her mind as controlled reverie. This inclination to reverie her daughter shares to a certain extent.
Curiously enough, Mrs. Mooney's thoughts yield a deter-
ministic argument. The outcome of her pondering over
the problem is implicit in her feeling of her power over
the boarders. In her deliberation, in her precise analysis
of the odds and evens of possible actions, we sense "property" shading off into propriety as legalistic equity modifies
her acquisitive temper and dominates the tenor of her
mental process. Behind this cunning introspection, one
can detect a concealed urge to revenge herself on the male
species. In her putting away of sugar and butter, we feel
her wish to "put away" her daughter by capturing Doran,
just as she had disposed of and dispensed with her husband. Indeed, she allows Polly to flirt. Although there
has been no open complicity, silent agreement prevails
between them.

After her rational weighing of factors in the case, Mrs.
Mooney pulls herself together with a resolute physiognomy:
"Nearly the half-hour! She stood up and surveyed herself
in the pier-glass. The decisive expression of her great
florid face satisfied her and she thought of some mothers
she knew who could not get their daughters off their
hands."

There, casually as though it slipped from her tongue,
the narration insinuates a reductive judgment of Mrs.
Mooney's praiseworthy, respectable intention. Does she
really want to get even with her husband by ensnaring
Doran? Reparation becomes the obverse of separation as
her thoughts tend to reflect the analogous fate of the
butcher's daughter, the great crisis in her personal history:
"There must be reparation made in such case. It is all
very well for the man: he can go his ways as if nothing
had happened, having had his moment of pleasure, but
the girl has to bear the brunt. Some mothers would be
content to patch up such an affair for a sum of money;

she had known cases of it. But she would not do so. For her only one reparation could make up the loss of her daughter's honour: marriage."

Mrs. Mooney has all the moral reasons to ask redress for her grievance; and she will have to act firmly because none of the young men, she suspects, mean "business." She wants objective accounting of the case: she counts all her cards. She purges all shadow of doubt from her mind as she looks forward, with assured righteousness, to a quick reckoning. Outwardly passive and shy, her cool mind hardly rattled, she will assert her own sense of justice. The decisive expression of her florid face, that of pleasure in the foreseen satisfaction of realizing her will, predicts the success of her cleverness in handling "the cleaver" with delicate skill. An expert in tact and tactics, she will conform to mores in order to advance her maternal pride.

Like a crafty artist, Mrs. Mooney knows all about the strategy of preparation, reversal, and timely denouement. She allows Polly's affair with Doran to culminate to where she can bring all the possibilities of her position as mother (and subconsciously as wronged wife) to the desired fulfillment. Thus, the setting of the story presents a spectacle which, with Mrs. Mooney as the vantage point of consciousness, becomes a concrete scene where conflict develops. The ritual of confrontation occurs felicitously on a calm Sunday, with its associations of pious morality, public exposure, and penitence. By metonymic tying-up, the following description of interior and exterior landscape projects a purpose objectified in the sensible surface of the world. Appearances of objects interact to produce atmosphere, elevating impressions to the realm of metaphoric significance:

It was a bright Sunday morning of early summer promising heat, but with a fresh breeze blowing. All the windows of the boarding house were open and the lace curtains ballooned gently towards the street beneath the raised sashes. The belfry of George's Church sent out constant peals and worshippers, singly or in groups, traversed the little circus before the church, revealing their purpose by their self-contained demeanour no less than by the little volumes in their gloved hands.

Before Mrs. Mooney confronts Doran, the "sacrificial beast," in a private interview, Joyce shifts narration to a view of the outside: the gay mood, the constant church peals from George's church (the chivalrous rescuer-knight offers ironic contrast), the gloved worshipers before the circus. "Circus" hints irreverent fun, contrasting with the "self-contained demeanour" of the pious. Polly and Doran's wedding, their union, is subtly implied. Sunday morning preludes the happy outcome of the confrontation: the day promised heat, a "fresh breeze" blew through the open windows, the curtains "ballooned towards the street beneath the raised sashes." Polly's confession lets everything out. Now the mother grasps at the right moment for springing the trap. For her this is simply a part of ordinary mundane life.

With the characterization of Mrs. Mooney setting the conditions and terms—the limits and possibilities—for the development of the plot, we shift to the object of her designs, Mr. Doran. As antagonist he also acts the victim in this universe where the outraged female telescopes evasive male and derelict husband in one substance. Both men (husband and Doran) are easily managed by Mrs. Mooney. But woman and man are unevenly matched, and acute disparity of character is explicitly underlined by the mother's set face, her purposefulness sharply contrasting with the fidgety, nervous state of the man:

Mr. Doran was very anxious indeed this Sunday morning. He had made two attempts to shave but his hand had been so unsteady that he had been obliged to desist. Three days'

reddish beard fringed his jaws and every two or three minutes a mist gathered on his glasses so that he had to take
them off and polish them with his pocket-handkerchief.

His blurred and foggy consciousness (his glasses are
misty), his compulsive gestures, all lead to a point where
if he exercised his own will he would be obliged "to
desist." Character reveals itself in a linguistic consonance
here. "Desist" counterpoints Mrs. Mooney's determination. The reposeful procession of the churchgoers outside
heightens by contrast Mr. Doran's perturbation. It aggra-
vates his condition, enlarging his sense of being guilty,
pushing him to final acquiescence. The young man's
dilemma evokes our sympathy for his helplessness, in his
doom of "being had"—how starkly accurate the idiomatic
phrase for Jack's notion of his situation when one recalls
that it is his character—his thinking and emotional disposition—that fatally commits him to rectify the "mistake."
     Forced to choose, Mr. Doran anxiously awaits darkness,
evening—a living death for him. God-fearing and socially
conscious, he is overwhelmed by scruples. Meekly submissive, he is ashamed at the prospect of marrying into
a "low" family. His name (a linking of "do" and "ran"
—ironically he fails to escape this time) suggests a possibility of disentangling himself from a "hit and run" affair;
but not daring, he will risk sacrificing his reputation as
a playboy with guts. Fear will make him unable to shirk
responsibility; he would rather be punished. His background hardly makes him a man of the world, as Mrs.
Mooney believes: he pretends to be straight and intelligent; he is really a proper and conventional person who
eventually confesses to the priest. Polly's thoughtfulness
confuses him; Jack's face frightens him. His confession to
the priest, who magnifies his burden, parallels Polly's confession to her mother—but with different results.
     Instinct drives Doran to succumb to Polly's innocent

wiles; sensual response leads to delirium and disrupts his regular routine. His vision of success and his notion of sin resolve the paralysis of his mind. Just as he freely satisfied his desire, he now seeks the object of his desire in submitting to Mrs. Mooney. But pleasure is a vice unless he is married; virtue and honor require the sacrifice of selfish pleasure. Immobilized, Doran listens to Polly's desperate "What am I to do?"—a question that applies more to him than to Polly. His celibate's instinct, plus Polly's exclamation of "O my God," provides the needed push to resolve his indecision, further reinforced by his figurative "descent" and the sight of Jack's "thick bulldog face."

Polly, seen from the perspective of her mother's thoughts, is the cause of the action and the object of the decisions of others. Ultimately she reconciles the two processes of thought represented by her mother and Doran. Although there is no "tacit complicity," presumably, between mother and daughter, Polly's confession gives her mother the initiative, inducing her to amass arguments against the young man. One will surmise that her silence during the whole affair repeats the lull in the fight between her and her husband. She waited for the last straw, the homicidal frenzy of her husband, before effecting a breach and denying him everything. Mr. Mooney's fate, in retrospect, coincides with Doran's.

Polly's name supports the attribution of "wise innocence" to her. Her singing a bawdy piece (which aptly fits her), with her gray eyes "glancing upward" and making her look like a "little perverse madonna," contributes to her image as a flirt of the establishment. Mrs. Mooney—to worsen the malicious innuendo of the boarders —thinks her good for the business. Polly makes "a clean breast of it" to her mother, confirming the mother's suspicions. Innocent and yet knowing (she timidly taps on Doran's door), she cries, seemingly in distress, before him. Without rash violence, her artifice looks natural; she crucially enters the man's room just as he is faced with the need to decide which course of action he will take. Her presence is decisive.

Polly's limited awareness is mainly responsible for bringing about the resolution of her case. Unlike her pragmatic mother, she daydreams and relishes the memory of her sensual experience; the white pillow she stares at connotes her lost innocence. Plunged in reverie, she grows calm. Her anxiety gives way to excited, hopeful waiting; she adjusts her hairpin, intuitively assured of a happy outcome.

Mrs. Mooney's wise patience and the institution of the boarding house contrive Doran's trap, with Polly as bait. Mrs. Mooney's demand for justice is expected; frustration seems unlikely. Polly's expectation is inevitably fulfilled, expressed in the future cognized as a past event: "she remembered what she had been waiting for." Note the subtle preparation for Mrs. Mooney's summons in the authoritative command of Doran's boss, Mr. Leonard— "Send Mr. Doran here, please"—which the pious subordinate immediately heeds. With the success of her scheme to exact reparation, Mrs. Mooney proves that she can look after her own well-being without appeal to the male sex.

Sunday, the day of Doran's ordeal, begins the week with the promise of hope for a better life to the believer. But Doran, a vacillating middleman for a wine merchant, neither a radical nor a virile seducer as he would like to pretend, feels the pressure intensify as he goes down the stairs to answer Mrs. Mooney's call. Mrs. Mooney has dutifully kept in herself the lesson of her brief married life; and now she exploits her chance. Throughout, she manifests no uncertainty; without any hesitation, she allows no change in her personality or in the pursuit. A slow floodlighting of her situation prevents any sudden reversal. Knowing her past and the operations of her mind, we can reasonably predict her future actions.

Custom and ceremony, social judgment and convention, seem embodied in Mrs. Mooney. She fits her environment perfectly; the milieu she personifies dictates her course of conduct. Economic security and social acceptance result from adherence to the mores of the tribe. Yet, ironically, the characters in this story reflect the disintegration of Mrs. Mooney's family. Given her husband as a lost cause, her vagabond drunkard son with his soldier's obscenities, and her shabby house, packing rowdy, unwholesome people, Mrs. Mooney adopts tough procedures in dealing with Polly's case. She stands for orthodox morality in an ambiguous way. Her personal desires prevail; Mr. Doran, paralyzed, relinquishes his freedom and independence.

The boardinghouse itself affords unity of setting in serving as a microcosm of a stable society based on the sanctity of contracts like marriage, filial respect, and the like. It affords coherence to the varying wills and desires of people, sheltering as it does assorted personalities under its roof. It thus sustains a communal life, the complex divergent relations of experience, and the multiple inward changes in the characters. All these The Madam oversees. Marriage brings permanent settlement to one of the transients. As an institution, the boardinghouse affirms the need for human communication based on stable relations; the lives of the boarders are here given pattern or identity by the operation of decorum, the sharing of common assumptions and norms in the given culture.

With reference to the plot itself, the boardinghouse functions as a means whereby Mrs. Mooney can fulfill her aborted hopes of sustaining a family and preserving her image of a reconciling mother. It serves also as a stage where conflicts of individuals dissolve under the scrutiny of a comic intelligence, the narrator's. Providing a shelter for a group of shifting employees, the boardinghouse runs smoothly under Mrs. Mooney's supervision. Her imposing presence constitutes the basis for order.

She lends to quotidian chaos the unswerving direction of her will: "Her house had a floating population made up of tourists from Liverpool and the Isle of Man and occasionally, *artistes* from the music halls. Its resident population was made up of clerks from the city. She governed the house cunningly and firmly, knew when to give credit, when to be stern and when to let things pass. All the resident young men spoke of her as *The Madam*."

Joyce's use of language in this story underscores the ambiguity of motivation in the protagonists and suggests, by this method, the stages of peripeteia and discovery in the plot. The word "to cleave," for example, operates in manifold ways: it can designate 1) to stick fast or adhere, to be faithful, and 2) to separate, to part or divide along natural lines of separation. A dialectic pattern of ends and means is played out in the antithesis between Doran-Mr. Mooney and Mrs. Mooney-Polly. Faithful to the memory of her butcher-father, Mrs. Mooney "cuts up" and disposes of Doran.

She has no qualms when she is convinced of the justness of her cause. Her mode of behavior can be meaningfully associated with the image of the "cleaver": her husband pursued her with it; she handles problems with a "moral cleaver." Images of cutting or severance recur in her systematic rationalizations. (In another sense, "cleaver" refers to a species of bed straw having hooked prickles on stem and fruit. Recall the scene where Mrs. Mooney is portrayed sitting magisterially in her "straw armchair" before the dining table.) Another multivalent detail is the color red. Doran grows a three-days' reddish beard, its color harmonizing with that of the recurrent wine (punch, wine merchant, etc.). Extremely discomfited, Doran cannot hold a razor, let alone a "cleaver." The color appears again in the description of Polly in his room: "Her white instep shone in the opening of her furry slippers and the blood glowed warmly behind her perfumed skin."

In the end, Doran's "fall," his assent to what Mrs. Mooney wants him to do, has been made extremely probable by the development of the narrative. His choice of alternatives has been narrowed down and drastically focused, his path decided for him by his character in the process of responding to circumstance; his dispositions are gradually affected and changed by external influences. Polly's appeal and Jack's appearance leave Doran only one choice: to accede to Mrs. Mooney's demand.

Joyce employs a technique of concentration in which characters are defined by the gradual narrowing down of their power to choose. In a way, the past determines their present; their temperaments and personalities, inherited from their parents, determine their fortunes. Thus the narrative sets Mrs. Mooney as the prime mover of the plot and determines the sequence in terms, first, of her dominant, commanding figure in the establishment, and second, of the psychological reasoning by which she clarifies and makes certain the only plan Doran will be likely to execute. Polly's sentiments and Doran's wavering and final intuition of what he should do for his own good inevitably follow from the serio-comic characterization of Mrs. Mooney.

Part III
A Gentle Way of Putting It

8

A LITTLE CLOUD

"A LITTLE CLOUD" CAN EASILY BE ARGUED AS A FABLE, A
quasi-allegorical study in size and criteria of proportion.
With Joyce, however, literal measurement and correlation
include the sense of measure. His thematic preoccupation
deals with magnitude, extrapolations, point of view, ambiguous ironies, and theoretical encompassing of the broad
scope of human possibilities.[1] Ultimately, this story involves the idea of a scale by which one can judge and
counterpoint the distance between sets of values and
attitudes, or between two interacting forces. At first glance,
the characters tend to be highly schematized—elementary
types of human behavior. But on closer inspection, one
perceives a finely nuanced and precise interweaving of
symbolic meanings and implications. The action of the
story itself imitates a dialectic of attraction and repulsion,

---

1. In "The Background to *Dubliners*," *The Listener*, 51 (March 25,
1954) : 526–27, Stanislaus Joyce argues that "A Little Cloud" ought to
be read as "nothing more" than a simple story about matrimony, "with
the figure of a successful and impenitent bachelor in it to cause discord
and cast a little cloud over married life." But the existing interpretations of the story run counter to that simplistic advice: see, for example,
Hugh Kenner, *Dublin's Joyce* (Boston: Beacon, 1962 reissue) , pp. 56–57;
William York Tindall, *A Reader's Guide to James Joyce* (New York:
Noonday Press, 1959) , pp. 26–28.

with a series of reversals that issue in inchoate recognition and suffering. The word "infatuated" affirms the pre-adolescent quality of Little Chandler's thought and its domination by infantile prepossessions; aptly enough, his child at the end overpowers him. The total build-up of incidents—happenings embodied in memory, observation, and longing—can be charted in a rhythm which proceeds from indifferent humility to communion with true self through a sense of futility and humiliation. Little Chandler begins with ambition and ends in acquiescence.

To present the character's trapped existence and his inability to respond with sensible decorum to the circumstances of life, the narrative assumes the pattern of a spiritual journey of a character in search of exact definition of identity by means of overt acts brought about by self-revealing decisions. These choices grow out of the character's predispositions—his cowardly temperament and his estranged awareness. The opening paragraph, which suggests Little Chandler's self-esteem on account of his friend's success, indicates the controlling attitude and the major flaw of his personality. His acceptance of his friend's invitation and the reasons behind it furnish the principal motivation for the plot.

Character, then, displays the pressure of the complete action of the story by its ethos, by its primary effort to formulate decisions. In the detailed description of physical appearance, habits, and manners, we discern the total physiognomy, the essential self, of the chief personage:

> He was called Little Chandler because, though he was but slightly under the average stature, he gave one the idea of being a little man. His hands were white and small, his frame was fragile, his voice was quiet and his manners were refined. He took the greatest care of his fair silken hair and moustache and used perfume discreetly on his handkerchief. The half-moons of his nails were perfect and when he smiled

you caught a glimpse of a row of childish white teeth.[2]

Note that he is not actually "little"; rather "he gave one the idea of being a little man." Juxtapose his portrait with his impression of Gallaher and there appears a symmetrical yet incongruous pattern which, from one angle, may be considered antecedent (Little Chandler) and consequence (Gallaher) of one argument or theme. We foresee the result of his excited determination to transform his talents into ample evidence of his distinction.

This trend of thought is elaborated in the three succeeding paragraphs, where Little Chandler's process of reflection forecasts with strict accuracy, by flashbacks and flashforwards, how he will behave with Gallaher and later with his own family. Thoughts of the past heighten by contrast the finitude of his situation. He believes that eight years have changed Gallaher from that "shabby and necessitous guise" under which he had known him into a "brilliant figure." Reinforcing his unrealistic assumptions about Gallaher, the lambent glow of the landscape mirrors Little Chandler's nostalgic, contemplative mood:

He turned often from his tiresome writing to gaze out of the office window. The glow of a late autumn sunset covered the grass plots and walks. It cast a shower of kindly golden dust on the untidy nurses and decrepit old men who drowsed on the benches; it flickered upon all the moving figures—on the children who ran screaming along the gravel paths and on everyone who passed through the gardens. He watched the scene and thought of life; and (as always happened when he thought of life) he became sad. A gentle melancholy took possession of him. He felt how useless it was to struggle against fortune, this being the burden of wisdom which the ages had bequeathed to him.

2. All references are to the Compass edition of *Dubliners* (New York: Viking Press, 1969).

The key words here—"fortune," "wisdom," "bequeathed"
—predicate a rationalization of present circumstance as
better than any alternative state, glorifying it as some kind
of inheritance, and so justifying in an ironical way his
later feeling of being a "prisoner for life."

To prepare the meeting between the two friends, in
which the actual scene becomes not so much a logical outcome as a subverting influence on Little Chandler's hopes,
Joyce loads his background material with overlapping
reminiscences, delivering affective information which
foreshadows Little Chandler's inevitable defeat. But the
objective tone claims authority for giving us something
more than the restricted consciousness of the main character. For his past life contains a twofold significance: it is
irreparably past, finished; yet our knowledge of it must
pass through the revivifying catalyzer of a present act of
remembrance. At the foreground of the action, we find
Little Chandler's hope for the fulfillment of his desires.
It is inspired by promises avowed in the past; it is evoked
by a painfully acute sense of difference between ugly
actuality and the felicitous richness of the imagination.

The transition from a scenery dense with romantic
properties ("a shower of kindly golden dust" veils the
unsightly aspects of the gardens) to the character's perva-
sive melancholy represents the typical movement of each
scene. Nature, seen through Little Chandler's eyes, con-
ceals the crude surface and sharp contours of things. The
narrative then focuses on the protagonist as he leaves his
office (the "feudal arch of King's Inn" evokes the image
of a medieval court, with Little Chandler as mock cav-
alier) and, by a technique of simultaneous reference, hints
of the discrepancy between consciousness and external
phenomena. With the golden sunset fading and the sordid
texture of reality thickening, Little Chandler diverts his
attention from the "grimy children" squatting like mice
and "vermin-like life" to the glamorous meeting place.

Ironically, Joyce adds: "No memory of the past touched him, for his mind was full of a present joy." The restaurant Corless, like the bazaar *Araby* in the story "Araby," serves to betray his sublimating, retrospective orientation: the ladies, "escorted by cavaliers," had powdered faces, and "they caught up their dresses when they touched earth, like alarmed Atalantas." Earlier we saw the aspect of nature colored by autumnal ripeness, externalizing subjective fancies. Now the unsteady, fleeting gleam of afternoon vanishes; the faint beams of evening that illumine the surroundings disguise the drab monotony of Little Chandler's life. Time releases the punctilious, reserved "knight" from subservience to authority, from meek serfdom to a static order and petty complicity with legal verdicts on man's freedom and fate.

And yet Little Chandler somehow discerns behind the ornamental glow surrounding the gardens the sterile, decrepit old men, "gaunt spectral mansions," "dear dirty Dublin." His discreet passion for neatness induces the protest of ignoring the untidy children and their natural, spontaneous vigor. Pondering his being ensnared by mundane life, he wistfully blames his environment. Dispatched like a questing knight, he quells the impulse of rebellion against circumstance and plunges into sentimental musings: "He stepped onward bravely." But these reveries, occasioned by vicarious participation with Gallaher's false dignity, stir up dreams and unbalanced assessments. His self-centered, morbid sensibility fails to yield any feeling of security and instead compels him to withdraw from active engagement. He evades sincere confrontation: "It was his habit to walk swiftly in the street even by day and whenever he found himself in the city late at night he hurried on his way apprehensively and excitedly."

Little Chandler admires his friend's success, Gallaher's bold face summoning "a slight flush of pride to his cheek" and arousing a feeling of superiority. But even his revolt is calculated with melodramatic distortion: "As he crossed Grattan Bridge he looked down the river towards the lower quays and pitied the poor stunted houses. They seemed to him a band of tramps, huddled together along the river-banks, their old coats covered with dust and soot, stupefied by the panorama of sunset and waiting for the first chill of night to bid them arise, shake themselves and begone." By a twist of imagery, night awakens Little Chandler from his drugged sleep and his obsessions, just as his reading of Byron's verse toward the end of the story provokes his child into frenzied crying, awakening the father from self-delusive stupor. The analogy is further strengthened by Joyce's motif of infantilism: "the thought that a poetic moment had touched him took life within him like an infant hope."

At the moment of his passage across the bridge, he seems to have intuitively grasped part of his inner self. Ambition and pride free him from timorous disdain of his environment, from his peripheral wanderings, his forays in filthy outskirts. The crossing harmonizes with a change of mood, his inflated hopes evolving into genteel pretense summed up in his wish to alter his name to "T. Malone Chandler." But the fake note would simply underline his womanish, conceited isolation.[3] The catalogue of his attributes cited above indicates a person lacking wholeness or unity; the "perfect half-moons" on his nails, in accord with his lyrical meditations, suggest an inner incompleteness already hinted at by his nursing an "infant hope" of success (he shows himself utterly incapable of nursing his own child), which proves abortive in the end.

At this juncture, this minor clerk of King's Inn arrives at the zenith of his dream-life and is therefore ripe for

---

3. On Little Chandler as "failed artist," cf. James Ruoff, "'A Little Cloud': Joyce's Portrait of the Would-Be Artist," *Research Studies of the State College of Washington* 25 (September 1957): 256–71.

comic deflation. His name brings to mind associations with a ship's outfitter, a magisterial lawyer, a candle-maker, a dealer in miscellany. But this protagonist is flagrantly innocuous, possessing an ego neutralized by the diminutive "Little" and by Gallaher's patronizing reference to him as "Tommy." With a precarious gait, he enters the realm of wishful thinking, here objectified by the restaurant. For a while, he loses the painful awareness of his limitations. Recall his idealization of women: Atalantas, charming immortals pursued by mythical hunters. Identities coalesce with decorative masks. Serving oysters (suggesting inner self unlocked, perhaps) and liqueurs (a redeeming drug for Little Chandler), Corless—echoing "heartless" and "colorless"—functions as sarcastic foil; the scene becomes the stage for the alternation from indulgence to reproof, the cycle of reversal displayed in his ruminations. An instance of the technique of undercutting illusions is the use of a style which Joyce describes as one of "scrupulous meanness," its fidelity to fact operating as a satiric device to purge the romantic who is confused by his own haphazard egotism.

The crucial dramatic encounter between Little Chandler and Gallaher—both anti-heroes in a sense—lies at the center of the narrative. But it is only a means of generating the crisis conceived as a realization by Little Chandler of the corruptions in his outlook, his faults, which he wrongly ascribes to the paralyzing circumstances of his life. The careful progression of effect leads to the epiphanic moment when Little Chandler loosens up and dissolves: "tears of remorse started to his eyes." But before this event, somewhat a formulaic denouement in *Dubliners,* Joyce's handling of situation and response has already adjusted the rhetorical impact, the tension between feeling and object, so that the pathetic fate of the character is not unduly forced on us as a foregone conclusion. The ironic

method of depicting character in setting and the oblique
contrasts between scene and psychological expectation
make the ending come off with a fine ordonnance.

The whole sequence of the conversation, composed
largely of Gallaher's talk prompted by his listener's susceptibility, outlines the course leading to Little Chandler's
gradual discovery of the truth about himself—a reversal
moving toward the final recognition in the last scene. The
opening paragraph has already provided the material to
be tested and elucidated by personal experience:

> Eight years before he had seen his friend off at the North
> Wall and wished him godspeed. Gallaher had got on. You
> could tell that at once by his traveled air, his well-cut tweed
> suit, and fearless accent. Few fellows had talents like his
> and fewer still could remain unspoiled by such success. Galla-
> her's heart was in the right place and he had deserved to
> win. It was something to have a friend like that.

The impressions are registered impersonally. But we
learn that this is Little Chandler's appraisal: he values
Gallaher's friendship in a subtly condescending way. His
speculations, though cautious and wayward, are sympathetic. The distinction between appearance and reality,
which he has so far shrunk from making, is clarified when
we see Gallaher later, his general impression now par-
ticularized with telling, selected features:

> Ignatius Gallaher took off his hat and displayed a large
> closely cropped head. His face was heavy, pale and clean-
> shaven. His eyes, which were of bluish slate-colour, relieved
> his unhealthy pallor and shone out plainly above the vivid
> orange tie he wore. Between these rival features the lips
> appeared very long and shapeless and colourless. He bent his
> head and felt with two sympathetic fingers the thin hair
> at the crown.

His "colourless" lips match the location (Corless), the

microcosm of Little Chandler's ambiguously discomfiting "dream-world," where Gallaher feels at home. Opposing images—passionate red and exuberant green—combine with sexual innuendos and the influx of raw sensations to intensify Gallaher's rakish bravura. His stampeding voice acutely contrasts with Little Chandler's pious awe. Gallaher, a boasting boor and consistent liar, reveals his unstable emotional state in his nervous tone and abrupt motions.

The two friends are counterparts in various ways: their names rhyme; both lack courage and fear the complex responsibility of life. Gallaher, though aggressive and articulate, is basically the same wastrel of eight years ago. Little Chandler, parochial and prudish, nourishes puerile ambitions that reflect his unruly mind. Gallaher hides his insecurity behind flimsy sophistication; his past, the "shady affair," and his gambling belie his virile-sounding, cosmopolitan wit. His vulgarity disenchants Little Chandler, nullifies his wonder, and suspends his planned exodus. Observe further how the ardently practical Gallaher, deficient in intellect, dominates physically, while his frail counterpart withdraws to mesmerized introspection. But the primary interest and purpose of the story are not, of course, the mere contrasting of humors, but the dramatization of clashing forces and values, whose unity is for the moment concealed only to be fully defined as the complications unravel.

Keyed to the tempo of middle-class life, the narrative pace accelerates during the meeting at Corless, exposing felt insights as embodied in the skillfully rendered sequence of action and speech. Joyce's shaping of structure affords the smooth rhythm of development maintained in the running parallelism between infinite wants and limited opportunities that finally culminates in Little Chandler's personal crisis. Three situations illustrate the movement of the plot as motivated by the inner contradictions in the central character: the situations involving conflict with himself, with Gallaher, and with his family. Joyce stylizes the presentation of the conflict throughout, as, for example, in the recurrent note of discordance between what the character knows and what the narrative directly exhibits. If one traces the sequence of the conversation, a pattern of arousal and disappointment will clearly emerge. Moods and fortune change almost imperceptibly as the action unfolds.

The internal tension in Little Chandler may then be construed as the principal mover of the action. And as the disparity between alluring London and squalid Dublin heightens, the demand for a resolution becomes more and more urgent. The disturbance springs from Little Chandler's comparison of himself with Gallaher who, representing the desired dynamic qualities, elicits a reaction from the passive admirer. Stirred from his reveries, Little Chandler appears too envious at first to be discerningly critical of his friend's faults. Gallaher gives off an appealing aura, but he also casts a shadow. Having escaped imprisoning Dublin, he becomes Little Chandler's projection of himself in a dazzling future. Ironically, it is Gallaher's shadowy past that partly substantiates his attractive image. Little Chandler's limited apprehension and shallow judgment at first reinforce the antithesis between Gallaher as a symbol of liberation and Little Chandler with his atrophied life. But Gallaher exploits his friend's querulous naïveté and obsequious gullibility. He undermines Little Chandler's married life and the bourgeois comforts of its milieu, with its odor of decay. After his first whiskey, Little Chandler senses discord and feels "somewhat disillusioned." Gallaher's accent and way of expressing himself "did not please him." But he rationalizes his perception of the disagreeable: "But perhaps it was only the result of living in London. . . . The old personal charm was still there under this new gaudy manner." We verify here the accuracy of the clerk's early impression of his friend's "fearless accent," which is now qualified by a tone of cynical knowingness as he discourses on worldly manners.

Having debunked Little Chandler's precious institutions, Gallaher goes on to poison his friend's marriage as he inquires about "connubial bliss," and congratulates him for having a son: "Little Chandler smiled, looked confusedly at his glass and bit his lower lip with three childishly white front teeth." He dares invite Gallaher, nonetheless; but the latter "defers" the pleasure, inducing chagrin in Little Chandler, who then begins to assert himself, exultant with drink and cigar: "He felt acutely the contrast between his own life and his friend's, and it seemed to him unjust. . . . What was it that stood in his way? His unfortunate timidity! He wished to vindicate himself in some way, to assert his manhood." He reveals his sense of being oppressed by his marriage: "he was aware that he had betrayed himself." The shock of Little Chandler's recognition that Gallaher has been "spoiled" by success after all is, however, modified by the subsequent exchange when Little Chandler foresees nuptial bliss for his friend. Gallaher confesses his view of marriage as purely a business affair; this bold nonconformity outrages Little Chandler and prevents him from succumbing to the tempting belief that he could ever be like Gallaher. Even his own presumed success in this private sphere of "manhood" is denied.

Soon Little Chandler is confirmed in his suspicion that he is an absolute outsider to his friend's bustling secular triumph, even though Gallaher still persists in treating him as a privileged acquaintance. He forgets to mention his desire to join the London press, his eagerness to plunge into work there counterpointed by Gallaher's festive mood. But his hope of escaping from Dublin is opposed by the constraint of his limitations, crystallized in his name. Finally, when Gallaher turns down his invitation with swaggering flourish, Little Chandler's eyes slowly open. He timidly clings to artificial order, to the super-ficialities of clichés and platitudes, for now his escape is frustrated and his ideals have been violated by what he hears—rumors of immorality and vice sanctioned by the mores of respectable society. He realizes that Gallaher's impulsive behavior does not fit, and indeed destroys, his idealized conception. Unable to resign himself, he feels cheated, so that later the incident is not even mentioned at home, though we sense its effect working insidiously in his breast. His condition after the meeting is radically transformed: in his loveless home, his child's protesting screams evoke painful shame for his worthless vanity. His pursuit of his romanticized persona generates disquieting insight about Gallaher, the self he would like to be, but its stature now diminished. He suffers from the look at appalling facts, then his balance is restored; with the fresh knowledge of his limitations he humbles himself before experience. In following the reversal of Little Chandler's affection for his friend, from unquestioning approval to qualified disbelief and then to mute alienation, Joyce con-trives this dramatized section to conform to the formal organization of the story.

Back home, Little Chandler looks at Annie's picture and recalls his fond anxiety for her in the past. But the picture—a tawdry illusion that copies reality—framed in a crumpled horn, initiates a repudiation of reality:

> He looked coldly into the eyes of the photograph and they answered boldly. Certainly they were pretty and the face itself was pretty. But he found something mean in it. Why was it so unconscious and ladylike? The composure of the eyes irritated him. They repelled him and defied him: there was no passion in them, no rapture. He thought of what Gallaher had said about rich Jewesses. Those dark Oriental eyes, he thought, how full they are of passion, of volup-

tuous longing! . . . Why had he married the eyes in the
photograph?

Dull resentment at the cramped quarters rises in him; with
his mind unhinged by the impoverished setting, his dissatisfaction increases. Just as his thoughts while crossing
Grattan Bridge had made him ignore his dismal surroundings, now his mood obscures the truth of his condition.

With mordant appropriateness, Byron's juvenile verses
disclose Little Chandler's anxious infatuation with heroic
fantasies so that while he is abjectly self-deceived, his act
betrays the profound discontent in his soul, evinced by
a melodramatic rhetoric venting his desperate, bitter disillusionment. (Byron the rebel later foreswore such gushy
stuff, attacking self-pity and hypocrisy.)[4] But while the
poem serves as fit vehicle for the theme of intimate grief
which kindles erotic passion, Little Chandler feels repelled
by his serious, distasteful wife. Ironical disparity between
his condition and the poetic content shifts to equivalence
when the resemblance between the beloved's tomb and the
dreary room becomes manifest. Virtually confined by narrow domestic routine, the husband evades the challenge
of critical reflection. The escapist recitation of the poem
advances the plot to the fatal, inconsolable recognition
that he is "a prisoner for life."

Now the child, who was previously taken for granted,
proves to be the father's master (his childish nature incarnate) and enemy. Unable to rebuke him verbally, the
child not only makes him ridiculous but also reduces him
to pitiful impotence. The boy's shrill presence, irking
the father and then jolting him into perception of his true
state, negates the maudlin pathos of the poem and affirms
the child's role as savior, the saving grace. He is even

---

4. Maurice Harmon, "Little Chandler and Byron's First Poem," *Thresh-
old*, no. 17 (1962) , pp. 59–61.

addressed by Annie as the sacrificial "little lamb of the
world," and "my little man!" For the child's paroxysm
shakes off the spell of illusions; his innocence precipitates
the weakling father into a humiliating retreat away from
his self-centeredness into the world of experience. Fear
smolders in the dungeon of his ego until Annie returns
to scold him fiercely and hatefully. Intimidated, he figures
as a little child. Unable to control his household affairs,
he miserably admits the defeat of his hazy ambitions and
shrinks before the angry wife who cancels his manhood.
The bullying father is overcome with futile despair and
becomes in effect the child that he is (recall his childish
teeth and effeminate look). This is anticipated after the
crisis of his meeting with Gallaher, an encounter which
produced all those complications now resolved in the final
scene. Tears, besides showing tacit self-condemnation, release frustrated desires and signify an awareness of de-
pendency on others. Little Chandler's shouts, a parody of
his "quiet voice" and "refined manners," are symptoms
of regret and an acknowledgment of guilt. Consequently
his remorse, subduing his once overweening pride, disrupts
routine and—in my reading of the story—conducts him to
a mature and viable adjustment to reality.

The narrative movement neatly rounds itself when
Little Chandler recognizes his true identity, his role
shrunken to that of a helpless victim. Extended interior
monologue conveys the direction of the character's limited stream of thought. Submitting to the force of self-
accusation, the paralyzing atmosphere of place, and his
own predictable nature, Little Chandler fails to establish
contact between his aspiration and its object. Speculating
on his dissociation from the depressing life around him,
he craves a transcendence that his will, emasculated by
vacuous daydreaming, cannot achieve. His lachrymosely
sensitive nature, which formerly could be stimulated by

drink and revived by the intrusion of an outsider, now
prevents him from rising out of his habitual ways and from
mobilizing his faculties. Unable to respect himself, his
spiritual thirst remains unassuaged. Forgetful, awkward
and clumsy, Little Chandler is afflicted by a lack of self-
knowledge; what he sees in Annie's photograph is actually
a reflection of his own petty, barren existence.

The title, "A Little Cloud," puns on Little Chandler's
trifling dilemma climaxed by the final outburst of tears
after the accumulation of "vaporous" longings. Earlier his
thoughts had begotten an "infant hope" of success, a cloud
obscuring the possibilities immediately around him, until
the child's sobbing startles his dazed mind and locates the
deficiency of life in his ineffectual self. "Cloud" may cor-
respond to the idyllic, remote world of beauty sought by
Little Chandler. Yet it also coincides with Gallaher's
"cloud of smoke" (parodying a saint's halo) which soon
dissipates. A cloud darkens: Gallaher casts doubt and
gloom on Chandler and also indirectly brings rain (tears).
On the other hand, Little Chandler himself may be the
drifting cloud presaging turmoil and renewal. Cloud signifies unfulfillment by its suspended state, and fulfillment
since it brings rain. (A cloudy firmament may allude to
the secret vital resources preserved in the inner self. In
1 Kings 18:44, the prophet Elijah beholds a "little cloud"
that foretells the end of moral and physical drought.[5]
Storm clouds concentrate as Little Chandler declaims the
verses relating the lover's visit to his beloved's tomb, which
the convulsive cries of the unwitting child disturb. He
glimpses the truth, the terrible irony of his situation. On
the whole, the cloud image functions as the focal context

5. For an allegorical interpretation of the story, see Harold Brodbar,
"A Religious Allegory: Joyce's 'A Little Cloud,'" *Midwest Quarterly*
(Spring 1961): 221–29. See also Clarice Short, "Joyce's 'A Little Cloud,'"
Modern Language Notes 72 (April 1957): 275–78.

of multiple references that fuse the plot with the framework of ideas, tying up motifs of quest, romantic revolt, affirmation, withdrawal, and so on. In the perspective of such thematic motifs, concretely embodied and tightly unified by the structure of the incidents in the plot, technical artifice and verbal play in Joyce's story acquire lucid, integral significance.

9

COUNTERPARTS

OF THE FIFTEEN PIECES IN *Dubliners,* "COUNTERPARTS" projects the most violent terminal scene, which irresistibly provokes the reader's partisanship. We would at once convict the cruel father for beating up his helpless son. We would without qualms always side with the child against the father. But to render justice to Farrington, we must never forget that his character acquires substance only as a function of the action shaping the narrative development. Without knowledge of the previous incidents, we would mistakenly judge Farrington only on the basis of his frenzied cruelty in a scene which actually discharges the cumulative force of the whole action.

Since a representational or mimetic work imitates action by means of the plot, the plot is the most important formal element in fiction. Plot denotes a system of actions; and system implies unity of effect based on the probability of a sequence of incidents. The incidents in "Counterparts" may be grouped according to place of occurrence: office, pubs, home. But these settings (the scenario) receive their emotional meaning from the incidents. Therefore we must construe the arrangement of incidents, the interaction between characters, in terms of a shaping principle sub-

ordinating the parts according to their ability to affect
the feelings and attitudes of the reader in the specific
manner contemplated by the artist.

The plot in fiction is not just a sequence of any probable
incidents but rather a sequence of incidents which effect
some important change in the protagonist, exhibiting a
power to move our emotions in a certain way. How is the
change in the protagonist of this story embodied in the
construction of incidents and their disposition?

Farrington's predicament begins with his failure to copy
the contract assigned to him in time—the reason why the
domineering Alleyne reproaches and punishes him. The
word *furious* conveys the tension of contacts in the beginning, tying it in with the end, when Farrington eclipses
Alleyne with his explosive condition: "His heart swelled
with fury . . . his fury nearly choked him." Because of the
intervening incidents, the change is not circular—a substi-
tution of exact counterparts—but spiral—more precisely,
an organic development.

The first incident contains probabilities which explain
the middle and end of the story. Probability depends upon
predictable causation: given a character with specific
thoughts and feelings, and the proper circumstance relative to his disposition and temperament, he will respond
in a specific, expected way. A brusque order first jolts the
anonymous man at the desk: "Send Farrington here!"
This sets the tone of the dialogue, punctuated with nasty
chiding. Communication by cries and abrupt gestures expresses the reduction of man to pure instrumentality. The
pattern of conduct adhered to by his superiors victimizes
the employee, who is not accorded a chance to behave like
a decent person.

Descriptions of Farrington at first tend to isolate him
as a nameless man in conflict with his environment: this
tall, bulky man hides his anger, curses under his breath.
He cannot express what he really thinks and feels. His

appearance masks his authentic self. Trapped by his own repressed nature, he cowers before Alleyne's high-handed impositions. He undergoes an idiosyncratic experience of sublimation, with feeling becoming translated into a physiological urge: "A spasm of rage gripped his throat for a few moments and then passed, leaving after it a sharp sensation of thirst. The man recognized the sensation and felt that he must have a good night's drinking." This reveals how Farrington's discontent will discharge itself in the time between his departure from the office and his arrival at home. Rage yields to thirst. Submissive in public but rebellious inside, Farrington does not protest: he sneaks out and satisfies his thirst at O'Neill's. But his stealthy game does not deceive Mr. Shelley, the chief clerk.

In inventing that particular incident of Farrington's covert escape from the office, Joyce is guided by two considerations. First, he wanted to show how the man's furtive, clever nature (intimated by the pastoral-innocence motifs throughout, e.g., his concealed shepherd's plaid cap) serves as a necessary premise for the protagonist's change from docile to suddenly defiant, and back to innocuous and meek. Second, Joyce wanted to maximize our sympathy for Farrington's plight and our admiration for his native resourcefulness. Moreover, Joyce seeks to display the causes that will motivate the character's choice: unable to satisfy his desires, Farrington, with a face "the colour of dark wine or dark meat," can resort to devious means.

Returning to the office, Farrington assumes "an air of absent-mindedness." The "moist pungent odour" of Miss Delacour's perfume assails him. Realizing the completion of his task to be hopeless, he abandons himself to paralyzing reverie: "The dark damp night was coming and he longed to spend it in the bars, drinking with his friends amid the glare of gas and the clatter of glasses." His mind confused by his drinking and enraged by its consequences,

he fails to finish his job. His subsequent frustration,
evoked by the mesmeric incomplete sentence he is copying
("In no case shall the said Bernard Bodley be . . ."),
appears a logical incitement to the next stage:

> He longed to execrate aloud, to bring his fist down on
> something violently. . . . He felt strong enough to clear out
> the whole office single-handed. His body ached to do some-
> thing, to rush out and revel in violence. All the indignities
> of his life enraged him. . . . The barometer of his emotional
> nature was set for a spell of riot.

The riot that will satisfy his nature becomes a reality later
at the expense of his son.

We must now inquire how, if the plot in essence shows
movement involving a change in the character's fortune,
this change is caused by the character's thoughts or doings,
as for instance by Farrington's sly drinking. Such a change
would either transform his former happy state to one of
misery, or vice versa; and it would alter his attitudes and
feelings accordingly. The change in Farrington's state
reaches a point where, after having been bitterly scolded
by Alleyne for hiding two letters (caused in turn by his
own desperately furtive practice), he "could hardly re-
strain his fist from descending upon the head of the mani-
kin before him." Given Farrington's temperament and his
dammed-up resentments, we perceive his energy somewhat released in a spontaneous but psychologically cred-
ible witticism. Retorting to Alleyne's rhetorical question—
"Do you think me an utter fool," Farrington quips: "I
don't think, sir, that that's a fair question to put to me."
This felicitous reply, a form of psychic aggression, catches
Farrington by surprise. He has almost succumbed to mechanical dutifulness, but his nature saves him. His personality both hampers and aids his dealings with others.
Often abstracted in his imagination, his instinctive self

expends its resources economically in a witty remark that his normal self, buttressed by the super-ego, would censure: "He had made a proper fool of himself this time." Determined by his conditioning in Dublin society, he retreats before Alleyne with an abject apology. His brief sensation of glory leads to his need to drink, compelling him to pawn his watch chain.

So far, the change in Farrington's state is from bad to worse. At first we see the origin of this change occurring in his thoughts, with his fortune not materially affected. With the aggravated sense of futility, his personality suffers a cleavage: daydreams obliterate urgent duty. Finally, with his witticism—the vengeance wrought by the libido—his fortune radically changes, with his personality and thought affected in varying degrees of shame and self-defense by rationalization. His thoughts strive to mitigate his humiliation by explaining Alleyne's hostility as due to a past incident: when Farrington was caught mimicking the man's North Ireland accent.

Nameless at the start, the protagonist of this story soon discloses himself as a sensual, easily inflamed man, whose reckless dissipation is later exposed in his journey from office to home. The stages in his becoming a bully involve an ascending scale of magnitude—from "Blast him!" to spasmodic rage, organic discomfort, and multiplied frustration. Although he succeeds in making Alleyne ridiculous, he does not escape becoming a laughing-stock. His ego injured, he wants to prove his masculine strength; lacking the opportunity, he invests his pride in the single retort. His thirst for esteem and recognition, satisfied in the pub (with Higgins's help), compels him to blow up his verbal feat out of proportion, omitting, for instance, the apology he was forced to offer.

The crucial incident before the last scene—Farrington's defeat in the trial of strength—becomes the terrible climax of his disappointments, especially because incidents of triumphant pride and heroic self-confidence precede it. An incident in the plot acquires a determinate moral quality (by harming or benefiting the protagonist's self or that of others) when it springs from a choice underlying the specific acts of a character. Consequently, Farrington's character implies the capacity to act or choose in such a way that the choice or act produces specific effects. We have seen that his suppressed rage and chagrin can be assuaged only by drink. The chief hindrance is his lack of money. But his instinctive shrewdness suggests the idea of pawning his watch chain. Prompted by the ache of his body for the comfort of the public house, this decision restores his composure and stirs joyful self-assurance; he looked on the crowd "with proud satisfaction" and stared "masterfully at the office girls." This condition destroys all residue of shame and regret, converting the cause of his apology to a proof of his virile intelligence.

It is clear that Joyce has conceived a plot that demands a character who will act in such a way that he will arouse a specific train of emotional responses. He then invents a character with just those psychic and physical attributes which will be most appropriate for performing the role required by the plot. For by means of the plot, the artist's purpose of arousing and gratifying a sequence of emotions is realized. Everything else—character, thought, devices of representation (point of view, diction, scale and number of incidents) —is determined by the controlling purpose of the artist as embodied in his arrangement of the incidents in the story.

We can venture asking at this point how we can formulate the organizing principle of "Counterparts." The kind of change Joyce depicts here involves a rhythm of unexpected success and anticipated failure objectified in a series of reversals. Farrington's ruses achieve nothing but his humiliation. Boastful of his witticism, he succeeds at the most in making himself the quasi-heroic protagonist in that otherwise shameful altercation. He falsifies the total situation of the clash between boss and servant. His hospitality in the pubs fails to ingratiate him with his companions. His need to be accepted by the group drives him through the process of stripping off all egoistic pretenses, including his claim of physical supremacy.

The whole revelry in transit from pub to pub cancels Farrington's individuality, merging him with the tribal or collective life of the city. When Weathers enters the scene, O'Halloran and Leonard exclude Farrington from their plans because he is "a married man." The appearance of the young woman with "an immense scarf of peacock-blue muslin," which recalls Miss Delacour and her hat with "a great black feather," leads to Farrington's vexed disenchantment: "He cursed his money and cursed all the rounds." Before he goes home, his expanded ego suffers deflation in the night's adventure. It leads to a predictable confirmation of his frustrations; he loses his reputation for cleverness and strength. Humiliated by his losses, he curses vehemently. Revulsion diminishes the glory of his witty self.

One will observe how the gradual depletion of Farrington's financial means harmonizes with his dwindling aplomb. He moves from private reprimand to scolding in public, from threatened dismissal to reduction in the usurious pawnshop, where he is forced to accept an unfair valuation of his property. Seizing the chance to prove himself and exhorted to uphold the national honor, Farrington accepts the challenge. His loss can be explained by the greater vigor of the younger opponent and by Farrington's drunkenness and dejection. Moreover, the rhythm of disappointment accelerates before the competition. He persists in sustaining his flickering pride by stubborn resistance to his submissive disposition, but his defeat by Weathers marks the decisive phase in his ignominious decline.

After the deeper humiliation in the pub, Farrington ends up by failing as a father, unleashing his "smouldering anger and revengefulness" on his child. He vents all his dammed-up impulses on his frightened boy, a surrogate for young Weathers. Note how the sequence of Farrington's degradation follows inversely the size of his adversaries: Alleyne, Weathers, his wife and home, represented by his son. Farrington's leisurely carousing in Dublin pubs induces a sobering isolation, until he is chosen to stand up for Irish honor by virtue of his generous dispensing of drinks and by virtue of his reputation. Finally he is reduced in size, his image as cowardly victim worsened by his bullying. He tyrannizes over his child to purge his guilt feelings. This horrible wreaking of vengeance on an innocent child makes Farrington the more culpable, because it is now no longer a quarrel between two adults (Alleyne and Farrington, boss and employee), but one between father and son. The reversal of expectations convicts the father of sadistic excess.

The major change in the plot occurs in Farrington's fortune and character, for he becomes brutalized by his own hunger for voluptuous delights and his inclination to indulge in romantic dreams. Forfeiting his reputation, he demonstrates the effect of the change in himself by his irrational violence in the last scene. The force generating the change in him comes from Weathers, who represents youth, urban glamor, illusions. Weathers, as the obverse counterpart, stands for all that Farrington would like to be. I must emphasize, however, that Farrington's defeat becomes severely painful largely because of his expectations and flattering estimation of his prospects. His yearning for beauty, and for companionship and joy, complicates the change, since we appreciate such an ideal of self-fulfillment as is implied by that yearning. However willful those aspirations are, we can still identify with

them because Farrington's position is one we can understand.

Joyce's main character engages our interest and sympathy because the narrative distance between us and the
nature of the man decreases in proportion to his increasing disillusionment and his ignorance about the forces
oppressing him. Yet he is not an utterly contemptible character. Pathos diffuses whatever perversity of will impels
him to violence. We are drawn to the process in which
the tensions caused by his bitter acceptance of his limitations lead to a reversal in his fortune at the beginning of
the story. But although he recognizes the immediate causes
of the change, Farrington does not recognize the ultimate
reason for his feeling so vindictive. The consequences that
accompany the change in Farrington, and the emotional
development the change ushers, direct us to conceive of
Farrington as an agent influenced and moved by his wife,
by the social conventions governing office and public life,
by the religious and cultural institutions, and by the
alienating collaboration of these with inherited traits.

Fluctuating light and darkness accompany Farrington's
search for his manly role. Divested of money and his social
image ruined, he shuns the dim barracks of his house.
Having accomplished nothing and now plunged in desperate anxiety, he punishes his son for the offense of
letting the fire die. But the father is doubly responsible.
He lashes at his child for neglecting duty; he himself was
censured for failure to finish his copying. His outbursts
exceed Alleyne's profanities and warning, since Farrington translates his threats into acts.

In effect, Farrington punishes himself for his cowardice.
His inept handling of his relations with others results
from the clash between his inhibited nature and the magnitude of his expectations. He victimizes the child whom
he should care for. His reaction to his own sad plight, to

reality, betrays him into committing the very thing he detests—abusive use of authority. The impact of the last scene comes from the spectacle of Farrington's disclosure of the self he has always restrained, his irrational, diabolic self. This compulsive aspect of his nature leads to petty despotism, and his act as whipper testifies to the tormented inner psyche that, lacking any creative mode of sublimation or release, can express itself only in cruelty.

To determine exactly Joyce's intention in portraying his character in the last scene, we may analyze the counterpointed overtones and connotations in the manner in which he represents the incident. A frightening note resounds in the boy's wild screams, inviting further the father's rage. The boy's recital of the Angel's salutation reminds the father of his wife, Ada, whose ministry, unlike the heralding angel's, coarsens the husband's manners. The mother-and-wife is absent; she does not welcome him, has left the boy to his mercy. She negates the suggested presence of the Virgin Mary, the Madonna figure, invoked by the child. Strangely enough, Farrington's fecundity (his large brood) contrasts with his impotent will and Ada's thoughtless dereliction. In context, the boy's pleadings mock the efficacy of ritual. For the father, a victim of circumstance, the prayer would be a fitting benediction. Like drink to Farrington, the prayer affords the boy a means of escape—a bribe to his unrelenting chastiser. Farrington's uncomprehending wrath constitutes a spiritual hell for him. His son's prayer seems not "a fair question" to lodge with him. With the fire out and blessed peace absent from the family hearth, the boy's unheeded prayer signifies a promise aborted.

Joyce orchestrates the various opposing forces that contribute to establishing parallels and interlocking motifs. *Counterparts* implies both similarity and difference. Alleyne and Farrington, occupying different ranks, contrast physically. While the little man with gold-rimmed glasses moves with dexterity and speed, the bulky Farrington moves sluggishly. Both become furious; but Alleyne's seething anger is released on Farrington, while the latter, prevented from exercising his rage in the match with Weathers, victimizes his frail son.

Unlike Alleyne, Farrington in the last scene is not a comic fool but a ruthless tyrant. For while Alleyne vents his anger in ranting and raving, Farrington expends himself in terrorizing his child—an unmanly procedure. He does not then duplicate, but improves upon, Alleyne's negativism. Appealing to the authority of his partner, Crosbie, Alleyne threatens Farrington and outwardly succeeds in disciplining him. Indeed, Alleyne's question could not be fairly posed to Farrington because the latter, as meek shepherd (his mock counterpart), behaves foolishly. His "thirst" for a courage he lacks is not only figurative but literal: note his bungling his work and his inability to tell the truth. Physically impressive, he lacks ballast: his "Blast him!" signifies helplessness.

The last scene possesses layers of likeness and antithesis: Tom, the father's "copy," has neglected to keep the fire alive (fire suggests a wide range of associations: solidarity, warmth, vigor, etc.). The extinguished hearth intensifies the father's fury. Farrington loses money, prestige, self-respect. His gift of mimicry, used in Alleyne's case because of their racial incompatibility, operates as a taunting and scornful comment on his wife's piety when he mimics his son: "At the chapel. . . ." The boy's answers—from straight reply to promise—parody the father's obsequious "Yes" to Alleyne, with comparable if more terrifying resonance. Farrington's unmanly job of mechanically copying contracts proves ironical, for he himself violates contracts. His wife reflects his own habit of absenting himself when most needed. Like Alleyne, Farrington furiously lashes out—here, at his child—in a vain attempt to get even with the world. But he confronts a dead-end in his home: the child's frightened, frantic pleas mirror his futile efforts.

The two problems the artist is challenged with in this story concern the management of the plot: how to combine incidents, character, and thought into a unified sequence, and how to represent the plot in language. For example, Joyce's handling of setting or scenario enables him to register social phenomena that reflect the inner world of his protagonist. The mediocre but attractive commercial world of Dublin inhabited by his protagonist does not offer any escape from the depersonalizing bureaucracy of the office.

It may be illuminating to point out how the pastoral motifs interwoven in the narrative texture with petty, corrupting facts create an inversion of the rural or idyllic tradition. Farrington's shepherd cap affords a disguise for his cheating. Bodily needs dictate the order of time. O'Halloran, in a banquet-like atmosphere, admits being overshadowed by Farrington's bumptious naïveté; the latter's own case apes the manner of the liberal shepherds in Virgil's eclogues. The allusion to Virgil's simple rustics and their mild speech, whose suffering from the deprivations of civil wars did not make them adopt citified barbarism, elevates the natural selves of these Dubliners to a level of dignity. We recall that Farrington is not even accorded simple courtesy in his dealings with Alleyne, who in turn is depicted as a weird automaton. Farrington and O'Halloran, like two provincials on a binge, brag about their verbal triumphs against the urban bourgeoisie. The wine that Farrington liberally offers as token of hospitality connotes the pure springs of a bucolic landscape. Even "Tivoli," the name of a pleasure resort near ancient Rome, reinforces the pastoral counterpart of this decadent world.

In a letter to his brother Stanislaus (November 1906), Joyce states that although he hates tyranny, as personified in the father's malevolence, he also repudiates the brutal atmosphere of homes where wives negate the man's desire for happiness. In general, women in this story serve to heighten Farrington's vanity and to tempt him with illusions of freedom and bliss. Snobbish Miss Delacour and the fashionable London lady represent that world of youthful dreams and carnal delight which would liberate the suppressed instincts and bring about contentment. Yet, as counterpart to Ada, the London lady indicts not only secular, utilitarian Dublin but also self-denying religiosity. Before these embodiments of passion, who extend the promise of involvement and redeeming union, Farrington, (like Eveline, and other Dublin denizens) reveals his impotence of will.

But surely this story is not a tract for improving marital relations. The returning husband's expectations seem implausible: he could not expect his wife to be a surrogate for the London lady. Ada does not greet him; his call is unanswered. A contrapuntal relation obtains between the couple: "His wife was a little sharp-faced woman who bullied her husband when he was sober and was bullied by him when he was drunk."

The meaning of "Counterparts" may be found precisely in the manifold reasons why the plot is constructed in the specific order the story has it, with parts magnified or contracted as the action demands, relative to the desired ends. In sum, the principle behind the deliberate structuring of incidents in the story may be formulated as an answer to the question: why does Joyce contrive the last scene in that way, making us pity the boy and loathe the cruel father, without absolutely denying us the feeling that someone else should answer for this inhumanity?

10

CLAY

THE ORGANIZING PRINCIPLE OF "CLAY," TO THE MAJORITY
of critics, may be deduced from the method used by the
narrator to place in the foreground the central symbol of
"clay." Cleanth Brooks and Robert Penn Warren, for
instance, argue that the "soft wet substance" Maria chooses
betrays her essential self and represents her destiny.[1] Sym-
bol-minded scholars declare that Joyce's intent is to portray Maria's character by metaphor and parallelism, by
the exploitation of allusions and objective correlatives.[2]
One should, however, realize that the artist practices discrimination. Each detail performs merely a subordinate
function in realizing a total effect. And the reader's emotional and intellectual experience, in its unity and depth,
measures the ultimate worth of fiction.

One must therefore insist on proportion in judging the
value of single elements, however recurrent or dominant:
the clay Maria touches indicates primarily the innocent
mischief of the neighbor's girls who misconceive her, with

---

1. *Approach to Literature*, 4th ed. (New York: Appleton-Century-Crofts
1964), pp. 137–40.
2. E.g., William T. Noon, "Joyce's 'Clay': An Interpretation," *College
English* 17 (Nov. 1955): 93–95.

due cause, as a suspicious, nasty, old lady. The use of the
piece of clay is a consequence of Maria's initial treatment
of the children. On this mimetic level, the trick played
on her—though capable of being associated with her pliant
nature and with death—demonstrates how circumstances
dominate Maria and compel her to act in ways that defeat
her ultimate purposes.

All commentators are agreed that the Hallowe'en party
functions as the crucial situation in which Maria's plas-
ticity and pitiful naïveté are revealed. Archetypal critics
enlarge immoderately on the mythical layer of the divination ceremony of the three dishes. They proceed to make
iconographical equations, such as prayer book=convent,
ring=wedding, water=life, clay=death. Marvin Magalaner even goes so far as to insist on a Maria-Virgin Mary
identity.[3] But clearly these allegorical classifications or
reconstructions only undermine symbolic structure (if
any) ; for if such details bear a one-to-one correspondence
with specific ideas, then we get flat, moralizing exemplum.
Hugh Kenner states that Maria's choice of death (clay as
death emblem) connects with her role as witch and ban-
ished ghost; "she returns to Joe's fireside until cockcrow
on all Hallow's Eve."[4]

Such simplistic readings distort the narrative framework in which party, game, and song occur as parts of the
plot. By "plot" is meant the sequence of actions leading
to a change in fortune, character (ethos) , or thought, thus

---

3. Marvin Magalaner and Richard M. Kain, *Joyce: The Man, The
Work, The Reputation* (New York: Collier, 1962, reissue) , pp. 95–100;
Marvin Magalaner, "The Other Side of James Joyce," *Arizona Quarterly*
9 (Spring 1963) : 5–16. For clarification on details, see the following:
Norman Holmes Pearson, "Joyce's 'Clay,'" *Explicator* 7 (Oct. 1948) , item
30; G. Ralph Smith II, "A Superstition in Joyce's 'Clay,'" *James Joyce
Quarterly* 2 (1965) : 133–34; S. A. Cowan, "Joyce's 'Clay,'" *Explicator* 23,
(1965) : item 50; Don Gifford, *Notes For Joyce* (New York: Dutton,
1967) , pp. 53–54.
4. Hugh Kenner, *Joyce's Dublin* (Boston: Beacon ed., 1962) , p. 58. Cf.
Richard Carpenter and Daniel Leary, "The Witch Maria," *James Joyce
Review* 3 (Feb. 1959) : 3–7.

arousing emotions proper to the appreciation of the whole form.

Now while Joyce may have sought to create in us an impression of Maria's childlike, ineffectual presence, this impression results from the total interaction of all the persons and objects comprising the world to which Maria responds by adaptation. She is thus not a caricature but a realized character within the plot. In composing the action of the narrative, Joyce employs Maria as the agent whose disposition, feelings, and thoughts lead her to choose (or to yield her will, still a form of choice) and decide in such a way that we acquire an insight into her existential being. But the function of character in fiction is determined by the subsuming sequence of events, the plot, designed to produce a definite sequence of mental and emotional responses in us.

We perceive the significance of character (or ethos, the power to choose and act in a morally determinate way) as a formal element in fiction when we grasp the action for which it was invented. True enough, the point of view or narrative voice Joyce assumes commands priority in explication. It is puzzling, however, to find one interpreter delineating two Marias—the heroic saint and the sterile witch—combining narrow piety, ideals, arrested virtue, aborted potentialities.[5] On the whole, the critics' verdict on Maria is divided: she is either morally culpable, or she is a pathetic victim of her society, of her inborn traits, or of something else. This ambiguous portrayal, a triumph of narrative authority to some, can be resolved by an elucidation of why events are arranged in the sequence we find; why a character with such thoughts and feelings behaves in just such a fashion in relation to what comes before and what comes after.

Point of view in fiction may best be considered as a

5. Florence Walzl, "Joyce's 'Clay,' " *Explicator* 20 (Feb. 1962) : item 46, reprinted in *Twentieth Century Interpretations of Dubliners*, ed. Peter K. Garrett (Englewood Cliffs, N.J.: Prentice-Hall, 1968) , pp. 107-9.

technique of representation dictated by the nature of the material and the kind of emotional experience the artist wants to arouse. In describing the spiritual afflictions (paralysis, pride, etc.) of his Dubliners, Joyce claimed that his style of "scrupulous meanness" reflected both exactitude and understanding. His manner of handling idiom and setting, summary and scene, is oriented to the end of mediating ugly or repulsive facts in a progressive revelation enacted in the plot. Revelation implies an ability to comprehend motives and to sympathize with the characters. The artist foreknows the ending in the beginning and the middle of his artifice. Thus, while the mode of unfolding Maria's past and future by dramatic close-up of her present conduct is supposed to approximate her sensibility, Joyce would like us to preserve the distance required to gain a just perspective on her and reach a balanced appraisal of her fortune in the particular segment of her life presented here. This distance is accomplished by objective narration, by subtle comment, by imagery and tone, by disparity in thought and deed.

Appearances tend to deceive in the fictional universe of *Dubliners*, concealing reality behind plausible masks. We must adjust our focus in order to connect abstract patterns of meaning, extrapolated themes, with their concrete specifications. In our estimate of Maria's predicament, how decisive the instrument of vision is may be observed in the disposition of her carefully prepared barmbracks: "These barmbracks seemed uncut; but if you went closer you would see that they had been cut into long thick even slices and were ready to be handed round at tea." Maria's muted, selective response to her world demands a closer look. Otherwise, seeing ourselves mirrored in those "big copper boilers" at the bewitching time of All Hallow's Eve, we forget altogether the obligation to maintain the superficial order of life—in itself a delicate, exacting responsibility.

Most critics have registered difficulty in identifying their

interests when Maria is regarded as a mere function of
realistically conceived situations. Her fatalism, her surrender of subjective will to external forces, rationalizes
our distance from her. We can then be critical or scorn-
fully amused without necessarily ridiculing the object of
judgment. The first eight paragraphs dealing with Maria's
grotesque features, her background, and her assessment
of her position quickly alienate most readers. Observe that
her actions are largely conditional, depending on the
pleasure of others. But this dependence follows from her
own feeble rationalizations (e.g., Protestants are serious
but genteel). This habit of finding disagreeable things
qualified or neutralized by likable aspects, testifies to
Maria's resilience and degree of susceptibility. Compromise distinguishes her evaluation of facts and her acceptance of her surroundings. Such acceptance, however, does
not imply acquiescence or abject servility: e.g., her attempt
to restore cordiality between Joe and Alphy. Her self-
respect derives from constant reserve, from "quaint affections" rooted in habit, piety, and discipline. She tolerates
flattery and teasing vulgarity because she feels a little
above the fallen but reclaimed women in the establishment. Accustomed to answer "soothingly" in categorical
fashion, and prudently methodical, she exhibits a yielding
stance throughout.

The attribution of a role to Maria, not as servant or
nurse but as "peacemaker" or mediator, foreshadows the
evolving curve of the plot and directs us to the calculated
development of the middle and the end. Abstractly put,
the argument of "Clay" centers on the domination of
events over consciousness. It concerns the clash between
good will and intellect, the thwarting of the will by an
unpredictable future. Contingency governs Maria's attempt to be faithful to her image as reconciler. From
the moment we see her undergoing the embarrassments
of shopping to her receiving the impact of Joe's refusal

to make peace with his brother, we exercise a generous but restrained sympathy for her. She is a doer, not a passive object; what she does possesses a moral quality.

In the opening account then, Joyce has presented no reason why we should condemn Maria for stubborn simplicity, or, conversely, why we should completely approve of her notions. She appears as a limited but well-meaning person whose developing fortune we grow interested in, if not anxious about. The narrator solicits our intelligence by arousing our curiosity. Maria's character appeals to our curiosity, engaging our attention in many possible directions. We become accordingly touched, patronizing, fearful, compassionate, angry, and so on, as we accompany her. She will try to change Joe's relations with his brother. If she succeeds, she deserves it; if she fails (which becomes gradually probable), she will just be conforming to her image as "superintending" servant, abiding with the flow of things. The odds balance with her capacity to yield and convert difficulty into an element of her system. In any case, Joyce succeeds in the beginning in attracting our inclination to judge, to be for or against.

Maria's pilgrimage to Joe's house aims at specific and general purposes: first, to try to reinstate the past harmony between the brothers; second, to enhance the gaiety of the Hallowe'en celebration. In the first, she fails; but in the second, she partially succeeds. To prepare the movement toward these incidents, Joyce describes her adventure in the shops and on the tram, disclosing her capacity for self-denial and tactful adjustment: ". . . she thought how easy it was to know a gentleman even when he has a drop taken." Her reputation as "peacemaker" may be justified, but in context it appears only as the matron's charitable gesture. Supported by her modest feeling of superiority, Maria's sensible tolerance helps to pacify the quarreling women. Nevertheless, she has failed to preserve the familiar rapport between two brothers; hence

she is a failure even as "a proper mother." Nostalgic over
past solidarity, she decides to revive in Joe a love for his
brother. We see her persuaded to this task, first, by her
polite regard for the gentleman who, though drunk, be-
haved courteously; and, second, by her perception of the
humaneness of Joe's appraisal of his manager. But Joe's
attitude, though consonant with Maria's tendency to relax
her fixed opinions, hides a core of frivolous egotism.

Despite her reservations, Maria yields to Joe's invitation
to drink, thereby generating an effect contrary to what
she expected:

> So Maria let him have his way and they sat by the fire
> talking over old times and Maria thought she would put
> in a good word for Alphy. But Joe cried that God might
> strike him stone dead if he ever spoke a word to his brother
> again and Maria said she was sorry she had mentioned
> the matter.

This climactic moment Joyce deftly understates, to cushion
the blow felt by the solicitous "mother." It is the fifth
in a series of aggravating frustrations, later clinched by
the error in Maria's singing—an error plausible enough
for her easily befuddled spirit. Joe's oath disrupts the
main line of action initiated by Maria. After she commits
her mistake, Joyce manipulates the end by shifting to
Joe's sentimental reaction. With the Bohemian atmosphere
of gypsy love undercut by the tearful Joe's groping around
for a corkscrew, the narrative modulates to a slightly
parodic scene. Harry Levin misleadingly construes Balfe's
romantic melody as doing duty for the feeling, so that
"we experience a critical reaction, and finally a sense of
intellectual detachment."[6] The plain fact is that her song
induces in Joe a sentiment which exemplifies Maria's
typical effect on others. It reflects the dual function of

---

6. *James Joyce* (Norfolk, Conn.: New Directions, 1941), p. 34.

the song as ironic reversal of her actual state and as a healing or distracting balm to Joe.

The first of the two stages of the ending involves a modified view of Maria's character relative to her failure to sustain her putative role as "peacemaker" by trying to resurrect a long-vanished harmony between the brothers. Her memory has revived the past and has projected a future that would duplicate or mimic the past. It turns out that her rubric of "proper mother" dissolves into gratuitous compliment, a precarious testimony of the worth of her services. It even insinuates her responsibility for the antagonism between the brothers and for Joe's brusque and maudlin outbursts. If she ignores her responsibility, it is because she is possessed by scruples and taboos that inhibit her creative resourcefulness. (Note that she is a "peacemaker" only because others have liberally humored her moods or condescended to pat her shoulder.) Her presence does not prevent Joe from drunken bickering. Maria may be conceived in this scene as an agent of magical innocence trying to exorcise secular or evil spirits (Joe's hostility) out of the hallowed dead (the past). Yet her striving only guarantees the discontinuity of the past and the present, of hopes and actuality.

When Maria is "courted" by the elderly gentleman, she becomes so affected that she forgets her plumcake and leaves it in the tram—a loss which leads to the panicked accusation of the children and their subsequent prank on her. Her clumsy absent-mindedness irritates amid her thoughtful ado over others' welfare. Thus her own temperament constrains her to act an unresisting role, one that is quite probable, given the preceding incidents. Things are soon rectified by the decorous Mrs. Donnelly, who prompts Maria to a congenial posture. The reversal from clay to prayer-book establishes the relevance of moral categories (Maria's goodness) to actual practice (her reward). More significant is the fidelity of her image in the game (her blindfolded, coaxed state may be a trope for her whole life) to her authentic self as revealed by her recoil from Joe's negation of her effort to restore harmony. Her maternal instincts are thus repudiated. Her whole life seems to have been devoted to dancing attendance on the vicissitudes of time and chance.

In the second stage of the ending, Maria's compliance with the family's request proves her lack of self-assertiveness. Apart from her desire to please, her drinking contributes to her almost impersonal performance, made convincing in an atmosphere of superstition, masquerade, and horseplay. Her visit coincides with a suspension of normal decorum. In actual life, she is unable to perceive the genuine motives of other people or the truth of her situation. Her ritual of submitting her proud dignity to the game and the song may signify her allegiance to the human community subject to change and death.

Unlike most critics, I need not belabor the psychic meaning of Maria's deliberate or compulsive omission. With the past irrevocably given up, Maria moves to legend and fantasy in song—an elaboration of the illusion-reality motif explored by previous interpreters. I must point out that Joyce makes Balfe's music a vehicle not only for a discharge of repressed wishes or urges—as Robert Scholes and others propose—but also as a medium for establishing concord between her (what she stands for) and Joe, between her and his children, and between her and the unknown and intractable future.[7]

We perceive, then, in the use of clay and the confounded singing, an "imitation" of the larger irony or incongruity of Maria's situation. From the moment she consented to

7. Robert Scholes, *Elements of Fiction* (New York: Oxford University Press, 1968), pp. 66 ff.; Thomas E. Connolly, "Marriage Divination in Joyce's 'Clay,'" *Studies in Short Fiction* 3 (Spring 1966): 293–99; Phillips George Davis, "Maria's Song in Joyce's 'Clay,'" *SSF* 1 (1964): 153–54.

be placed in *Dublin by Lamplight,* she has accepted the
burdens and mixed consolations of life. Intuitively aware
of her weakness, she changes her opinions and readily
gives allowances, selflessly searching for the positive in
every negative. She tempers her whimsical reservations
with serious concessions. Because she lacks any ambition
and makes no excessive demand on life, she can resign
herself to the intermingled good and bad in experience.
She acts as a reconciling medium for the tensions in the
laundry and in Joe's family. Although we are ignorant of
her personal history, we can infer the kind of surrounding
that has produced her flawed sensibility. Devoid of ener-
getic will, she exerts a beneficent influence by allowing
the defects of others to expose themselves in their treatment of her. Her strong, blind trust in the forces operating behind the scenes, and her clay-like nature, permit
those forces to betray their limitations.

Richard Ellmann suggests that when Joyce shifted his
original emphasis from Joe to Maria, "the tone of the
story accordingly slanted away from irony to guarded
sympathy."[8] Joyce contrives to do full justice to Maria's
case: his satiric but balanced depiction of her whole self
displays a detached precision that illuminates her milieu.
His restrained report of Maria's actions is actually a passionate indictment of her milieu. William York Tindall
mistakenly assigns the "epiphany" of barrenness and chaos
to Joe.[9] (Unquestionably it is the reader who experiences
the so-called " epiphany.") Instead of probing into the
psyche of his characters, Joyce evokes interior processes
by emphasis on and isolation of telling, concrete details.
We must also recognize that no increase of awareness on

---

8. *James Joyce* (New York: Oxford University Press, 1959), p. 196; see
also pp. 18–19. Cf. Thomas F. Staley, "Moral Responsibility in Joyce's
'Clay,'" *Renascence* 18 (1966): 125–28.

9. *A Reader's Guide to James Joyce* (New York: Noonday Press, 1959),
p. 32. On the Joe-Alphy opposition, see Robert M. Adams, *James Joyce:
Common Sense and Beyond* (New York: Random House, 1966), p. 76.

Maria's part is needed for her to succeed in her role. The
clarity and candor of Joyce's style enable the surface texture of his fictional world to manifest a purpose which
structures discordant facts into an intelligible whole.

"Clay" stresses the importance of seeing a thing in
perspective, of recognizing the protagonist's identity in
the context of a world itself severely wanting. Maria's
simplicity, her saving grace, acquires substance and depth
in subserving the action embodied in the plot. The surface details provide enough clues for us to grasp the
writer's intention in composing an action for which Maria
is precisely the appropriate and efficient protagonist.
Those critics who fail to apprehend the sense of the whole
form of "Clay" as the imitation of an action would do
well to scrutinize the plot, where the immanent form
of experience—the raw substance or "clay" of art—is
rendered with integrity and radiance.

11

A PAINFUL CASE

THE FORMAL CONSTRUCTION OF "A PAINFUL CASE," AN extended alternation of description, summary, and action (the quantitative parts), is mainly executed by connecting qualitative elements—diction, thought, character, plot —to bring about a crisis and a recognition as a result of the protagonist's action. Mr. Duffy's action indeed consists of a refusal to act; and this refusal, by its moral effect, deprives Mrs. Sinico of any need to be a meaningful presence in his life. Her death (in an accident after an interval of four years) is required by Mr. Duffy's severance of all relations between them and his rationale about the impossibility of any emotional attachment between men and women.

Viewed from this reasoning, the accident may be explained as a probable incident caused—and meaningful only when caused—by Mr. Duffy's will to disrupt human interdependence, by his mechanical insistence on vain withdrawal and introversion, by his fear of life. And it is this fear of life which evokes our disapproval of his character, his complacent but inhuman resignation, until the news of Mrs. Sinico's fatal accident objectifies the "virtues" which he embodies—the impersonality and precision of his habits—and initiates in him a process of self-inquiry and moral judgment.

The central action of the story, then, consists of a single line of movement of Mr. Duffy's consciousness from ineffectual and sordid isolation to a growing awareness, after the partly "accidental" and partly willed involvement with Mrs. Sinico, of what that isolation means. The parts of the story add up by this principle of maintaining consistency of character. But characterization subserves the larger total effect of the narrative framework in which the protagonist's life, "an adventureless tale," acquires an identifiable wholeness. Thought predominates in the beginning, part of the "treatment" as distinguished from the "subject" (Henry James's terminology). Feeling disrupts the continuity of generalized portrayal when Mr. Duffy meets Mrs. Sinico. In the ending, thought begets its own annihilation in the internal monologue, with images and concrete particulars of time and place bodying forth the remembered scenes of the past, Mrs. Sinico's ghost determining the obsessive experience of Mr. Duffy.

The story, then, may be formulated in terms of a schematic outline: Mr. Duffy, assured of his vital powers, proves to be closely allied with the dead in the end. Mrs. Sinico, dead, is transfigured and incarnated in the continuing life of nature and man. But this demonstrated reversal hinges on Mr. Duffy's capacity to explain his situation, to make inferences about cause and effect, and to accept responsibility for the probable effects of his actions. The moment when he recovers from the shock of learning about Mrs. Sinico's death marks a change in his persistent stance of assured rectitude. It is both inevitable and surprising to find him examining his conscience at this point, because we have been prepared to expect this constant habit of introspective analysis, although now the inward searching leads to a negative, critical judgment of self.

At the opening of the story, Joyce establishes the likelihood for the affair with Mrs. Sinico with four paragraphs of specifics about Mr. Duffy's capacity for doing and suffering, his weakness for music, and the like. The occasion for the meeting between them is generally possible. One telling feature foreshadows the future break in the relation: Mr. Duffy's "cheekbones also gave his face a harsh character; but there was no harshness in the eyes which, looking at the world from under their tawny eyebrows, gave the impression of a man ever alert to greet a redeeming instinct in others but often disappointed." The association deepens, with Mr. Duffy initiating the move for further complication. His role as agent comes out with graduated involvement, from the *ad hoc* remark in the Rotunda up to the point where he converts accident into planned event: ". . . he forced her to ask him to her house. . . ." Her companionship, "like a warm soil about an exotic," nurtures him. Her redeeming spontaneity and instinctive responsiveness penetrate through his disguise and reveal, with the impact of her bodily presence, his extreme fallibility, his vanity.

Advanced by one part of Mr. Duffy's character, the intimacy inevitably yields to an assertion of his essential character: his surprise at Mrs. Sinico's passionate gesture and his subsequent disillusionment. His surprise stems from his blindness, his insensitivity to the needs of the other person (given the qualities attributed to him at the opening of the story). He is thus caught unawares by the current of passion his contact has generated in Mrs. Sinico. He begins a countermovement away from her until both "agreed to break off their intercourse. . . ." Irony undercuts his claim of an intimate bond with her, for instead of a "bond" one perceives merely thoughts "entangled" and egocentric opportunism satisfied in his conception of the woman as a mere receptacle for his ideas, a flatterer of his "discourses." Before he learns of her death, his *sententia* on sexual intercourse has already "sentenced" her to nonexistence.

From Mr. Duffy's house, the Rotunda, and then to Mrs. Sinico's "ruined confessional," the narrative moves in a cycle of isolation and withdrawal. No disruption of the circular development occurs; even Mrs. Sinico's affection is nullified or perverted by Mr. Duffy's paralyzing selfishness. Mrs. Sinico (her name puns on "sinecure," "sin," and *"sine coitione"*) seems driven by the void caused by her ineffectual marriage and broken home. But fearful that his inner vacuity will be exposed, Mr. Duffy, cashier of a private bank, immediately forecloses the relation: ". . . they agreed to break off their intercourse. . . ."

After four years, Mr. Duffy realizes his literal and spiritual bankruptcy. Life proves inexorably heedless, indifferent: his father has died, the junior partner of the bank has retired. It seems at first that change will not overtake Mr. Duffy, for his habits now intensify his former state, as though Mrs. Sinico had never impinged on his life. But his "third person" pose breaks down when he reads the news of Mrs. Sinico's death, his lips moving like a priest's in prayer. Communing with the past, he is able finally to conjure for a moment the woman's spirit in the Park, where the past afflicts him by juxtaposition with the images of lovers, tree, river, garden, and portentous train.

An interval of four years is needed to witness the stiffening of Mr. Duffy's character (note the reinforcement of his ego by Nietzsche's concept of the "superman") and the goal to which this hardening of attitude tends in relation to Mrs. Sinico.[1] For if we consider the cause of her death (as ambiguously related by the news item,

---

1. For the literary influences on the story, see Marvin Magalaner, "Joyce, Nietzsche, and Hauptmann in James Joyce's 'A Painful Case,'" *PMLA* 68 (1953) : 95–102.

"Death . . . has been probably due to shock. . . .") , we see that Mr. Duffy's logic, his negation of her offer and his reason for living alone is truly responsible for her death. Thus Mrs. Sinico's death, as a formal aesthetic "event" in the context of this fiction, is not oddly accidental but integrally necessary (the climax of the sequence of probable incidents) . Mr. Duffy is the "formal cause" of her death—within the range of alternatives or possibilities set by the framework of the action and the fortune of the protagonist as they are imitated by the plot.

The technical use of the newspaper report serves to objectify the impersonal, frigid self-sufficiency which Mr. Duffy has tried to embody in himself and his life, but which he now finds abhorrent. The visceral repulsion at the news betrays the core of his sensibility. Nonetheless, he justifies his outrage at the vulgarity of Mrs. Sinico's suicide. Devoid of sympathy, his mind wanders; in the pub, he plunges into a crisis of conscience: "He asked himself what else could he have done." The maxim "character is fate" is exemplified by Mr. Duffy's "painful case." But since character (*ethos*) , as said before, is manifested in the power of moral choice and the effects produced by choice, we must concentrate on the nexus of cause and effect, antecedent and consequence, crystallized in the working efficacy, the power, of the plot.

To formulate the organizing principle of the story, it might be useful to explain first the effective role and function of the news item quoted at the center of the narrative as a formal fictional device. Dividing the regular time-table of Mr. Duffy and the disrupted world which the item creates in his consciousness, the news sums up Mrs. Sinico's life, suggesting her futile efforts to establish a liaison with another man and the subsequent violation of her trust. Both the engine driver and railway porter disclaim any responsibility, intimating Mrs. Sinico's "fall."

Her "painful case" is clinched by the judgment at the
end which is applicable to Mr. Duffy's death-in-life "case":
"No blame attached to anyone."

With all his delicate refinement, Mr. Duffy feels revolted by the inert, hackneyed style of the report. The
obituary contained in the news, an analogue of Mr. Duffy's
platitudes, undermines his cold self-possession. His
thoughts generate an impetus to claim proud innocence
about the whole affair. He anxiously rationalizes his past
acts. His first reaction to the news registers his indig-
nantly righteous attitude; he feels degraded and defiled by
the woman's shameful fate. Yet the style of noncommittal
reportage objectifies his character with stark accuracy. It
exaggerates his apathy to a certain extent; but it displays
essentially the same tone and mode in which he conducted
his flirtation with Mrs. Sinico. The "accident" and its
description point to the "accidental" nature of their contact, and mock his outlook and behavior by parodic mimicry. The news serves as the diagnostic mirror of his
personality, reflecting by his own emotional response to
it his cowardly and suicidal plight. In effect, by its mode
of reenacting Mr. Duffy's abortive and nihilistic conduct
toward Mrs. Sinico, the report exonerates the woman from
all malicious charges and in turn convicts Mr. Duffy of
moral turpitude, of criminal negligence. He himself feels
shocked and intensely repelled by it. Otherwise implausible except as a device to trigger his awakening, his revulsion boomerangs: he is actually revolted by his own sordid
life. With accelerating nervousness, his memory fails as
in the park he recognizes the enormity of his guilt: he
feels his "moral nature falling to pieces." This sense of
culpability, however, results from a part of his nature that
he seeks to deny: his aesthetic sensibility. The dimension
of thoughts and feelings which constitute the groundwork
for choice, and which through the decisions and acts of
the character affect the development of the plot, may be

discerned in the recurrent modes of expression Mr. Duffy adopts. Recall his peculiar trick of referring to himself in the third person, with a predicate in the past tense. His self-righteous attack, a vehement invective, against his fellowmen and the country's culture attests to his remoteness from being moved to establish communication. His attitude assumes petrified shape in the dogmatic absolution of his logic as displayed in his belief that "love between man and woman is impossible because there must be sexual intercourse." Thus, on the level of thought and diction, the predominant indirect discourse of narration and the scrupulous registration of incidents contribute to bring into focus the continuity of the plot and show further the probable implications of facts and the factual result of the implications.

The ending pronounces judgment on Mr. Duffy's guilt. Accident becomes part of a probable progression of happenings. Joyce symbolizes the entire action in the transcription of surroundings and its effect on Mr. Duffy's consciousness. Self-castrated, as it were, by his strict asceticism, Mr. Duffy has denied himself the possibility of fulfilling his virile qualities, the potency of his manhood. Naturally "saturnine," he lacks warmth; he decides against achieved contact with a woman. (Note that the train that killed Mrs. Sinico is temporarily halted.) Mr. Duffy feels secure, like the railway company that officially declares its innocence yet apologizes for the catastrophe. As the report correctly says, Mrs. Sinico died from failure of the heart— from the rejection she suffered.

The last two paragraphs exhaust all the possible implications of Mr. Duffy's self-imposed "trial": the suggestions of alienation from the city and its communal harmony, the denial of love, his sensitivity and egocentric withdrawal, which are all rendered with graceful economy in the beginning. Structurally, the last two paragraphs epitomize the pattern of meeting, stabilizing of friendship and its heightening, and sudden break of the relation. The passage of the train postfigures in part the passage of a significant moment in Mr. Duffy's existence. The circular development of his life is telescoped in the statement "He turned back the way he had come. . . ." Habit surmounts the epiphanic instant: "He began to doubt the reality of what memory told him." Anticipation evokes "perfect silence." The concluding impression, "He felt that he was alone," reverts to the original situation in which it was concealed as premise or motivation for the action (see the first sentence of the story).

Submerged in the agony of self-pitying remorse, Mr. Duffy's spirit fails to recognize the harmony of the train's winding course with the river's winding progress through the city. Life continues, the rhythm of nature's growth goes on, the lovers in the park proceed in their procreative act. He apprehends the reversal of his fortune as he "gnawed the rectitude of his life"; now he recognizes that he himself has brought about the change. Given the nature of his role as effective agent in the story, Mr. Duffy's feeling of isolation, of being completely abandoned, becomes the inevitable and just ending of this period of his life.

To illustrate the whole-part interdependence and synthesis of image and plot in the story, it is sufficient to emphasize the powerful image of the train, which Mr. Duffy saw "like a worm with a fiery head winding through the darkness, obstinately and laboriously." The train may be said to represent death and the destructive unknown, or the force of the irrational as it betrays itself in fear and wrath. Mr. Duffy's "entanglement" with the woman leads to her death. By association the train acquires a negative connotation: it suggests the worm-like force of isolation and unreason that entangles and kills.

Apprehending the formal whole which the narrative sequence realizes in time, Joyce handled all the parts of

the work in a manner designed to evoke such emotional
effects as are consonant with his larger purpose. The final
cause or object of the narrative resides in the action represented: the action may be formulated as the process in
which the protagonist's innocence discovers itself guilty,
vain, and impossible. Our emotional responses follow a
pattern of initial perception of Mr. Duffy's state deduced
from the factual circumstances of his life, which is then
qualified with disapproval of his conduct in the affair with
Mrs. Sinico and of his vanity, which caused the estrangement. Our emotions pursue a sequence leading to a
reversal when Mr. Duffy's reflection on his superiority
gradually dissolves and is almost annihilated by his remorse, until our compassion for the self-condemned man
succeeds; we sense that his infernal solitude at least
betokens purgation and humility.

The development of the plot essentially assumes a
comic direction, modified in the middle by a sentimental
complication with a residual pathos: the character is
shown dominated, typed, by a humor or an obsession. By
describing the function of the crucial parts of the narrative, I have tried also to define the stages of our emotional
response to the character of Mr. Duffy.

One will observe how the parts of the story cohere in
a pattern rendered in dramatic sequence by the movement
of the plot; the plot is the basis of organic unity. The
power of the narrative structure inheres in the dynamic
continuity of the plot, translating contingent details into
probable elements in the action. The plot of "A Painful
Case" renders a whole sequence, involving the transition
from self-satisfied security which, though it generates
within itself its own contradiction, still preserves its blindness to its inner chaos until it is faced by its absurdity
when objectified in the content and style of the news
report. From then on, the spiritual resources of the protagonist heighten and vitalize the dialectic of defensive

pride, doubt, ennui, and despair, until the movement of his psyche—as disclosed in his thoughts and feelings, in his response to the news—evolves into subjective chaos and his intuited recognition of responsibility for the reversal or change in his fortune, his total condition. The whole of "A Painful Case" is the dramatic and rhetorical rendering of such an experience in terms of plot, characterization, thought, and thematic argument, which I have tried to elucidate here.

Part IV
Scrupulous Meanness

12
IVY DAY IN THE
COMMITTEE ROOM

AMONG THE CLASSIC TALES IN *Dubliners,* ONE OF THE MOST
economically conceived and rigorously executed is "Ivy
Day in the Committee Room." Unfolding the action in a
clear and, at first glance, extremely simple outline, Joyce
may have created a story that contains nothing of the
symbolic complexity and intricate depth of meaning one
finds in "The Sisters" or "The Dead." Analysis of the
story as it develops in chronological sequence will, however, make explicit some of the manifold ironic tensions
and unifying analogies that Joyce has subtly embodied in
the texture and pattern of his narrative.

The title of the story, assigning a specific time to a
particular place, indicates the narrative development as
climaxing in a celebration where the personages gather
in a single place. The place then affords unity of setting,
and the day the duration of happening. Two lines of
action are implied in "Ivy Day," namely, the commemoration of Parnell's death anniversary, and the political business entailed by the function of the room. "Committee"
and "ivy" connote opposing values, the public and the

intimate. A fusion of the two lines of action toward the end, when Hynes performs his "funeral oration," yields a spectacle of pathos and ironic repudiation. The action of the story is precisely defined by this unexpected turn or reversal from a concern over money to a reluctant awareness of values counterpointed by money. And the recurrent motif of money, a principal motivating force, stresses its fiat quality and the foundation of value on personal commitment (Tierney's word).

Old Jack, fire-provider and patriarch *manqué*, introduces us into the room's cryptic atmosphere. Permanently stationed in the room throughout, he laments the death of the old order. He is treated badly by his son, and receives scant respect from the adults (Henchy, for instance, grabs the seat he vacates). He grumbles about his son's drinking, but he himself is the culpable counterpart; he grudgingly gives a drink to the seventeen-year old boy with the corkscrew. Obviously he needs emotional warmth and self-knowledge, but the hellish-looking fire he tends provides neither. The fire simply flickers and never blazes, in spite of his efforts.

The elders—Old Jack himself, O'Connor, Hynes, and the rest—regard the young as unworthy of respect, the young being heedless of their despicable waiting for "a miserable handout." The patriarchal figure (familial, holy, city fathers) thus assumes the role of scapegoat-victim. When Old Jack lights two candlesticks, the hearthfire loses "all its cheerful color": the power of reality and death triumphs over the regenerating power of fire. Coals, either infernal or purgatorial, reveal the room's emptiness, the contortions and blemishes of faces—the ugly texture of spiritual poverty. Consider the description of O'Connor:

> Mr. O'Connor, a grey-haired young man, whose face was
> disfigured by many blotches and pimples, had just brought
> the tobacco for a cigarette into a shapely cylinder but when

spoken to he undid his handiwork meditatively and after a moment's thought decided to lick the paper.

After announcing the reason for his lingering (Tierney's return), O'Connor spoils the campaign card, a token of the trust placed in him: "Mr. O'Connor tore a strip off the card and, lighting it, lit his cigarette. As he did so the flame lit up a leaf of dark glossy ivy in the lapel of his coat." The betrayal of Tierney's trust and the accidental disclosure of what underlies this betrayal—Ireland's shameful betrayal of Parnell—are dramatically projected in O'Connor's telling gesture.

O'Connor's incongruous features (he seems to have been born old: "grey-haired young man") conform with his use of the candidate's card to light his cigarette. His unpleasant look is aggravated by his indecisive sloth, his lack of initiative and originality. Old Jack talks about his son's drinking and his futile attempt to arrest it. O'Connor's response affirms his inner lethargy: "Mr. O'Connor shook his head in sympathy, and the old man fell silent, gazing into the fire." The dull coals illumine the denuded room, which serves as witness to the electioneering and to the men's distrust of their employer. The condensed action heightens the moral paralysis for which, by assent or apathy, each of the men is responsible. None of these pitiable mercenaries fully apprehends the death of his spirit; all are caretakers in a ceremony that parodies or mocks the ritual for the dead. It is the reader who finally understands the possibilities of life that have been denied by the bondage suffered by the men, a fate equivalent to their character. On the whole, death and life wage war in the committee room, and the power of death seems to assert its ultimate supremacy.

With the stage set for the complication of the plot, Hynes enters and asks whether Tierney has paid up. Greeting the two men with "What are you doing in the

dark?" Hynes himself is "in the dark." The other characters are unable to place Hynes: Henchy suspects him
as a spy from Colgan's camp. Hynes defends Colgan the
Fenian and considers himself a plain honest man, a
patriot. The topic of conversation shifts from the payment
by Tierney to the comparison between Tierney and Colgan, then to Hynes's defense of Colgan, and temporarily
breaks off with O'Connor's feeble nod to Hynes's suspicion about "Tricky Dicky" Tierney and the first overt
reference to Parnell: "Mr. Hynes took off his hat, shook
it and then turned down the collar of his coat, displaying,
as he did so, an ivy leaf in the lapel. 'If this man was
alive,' he said, pointing to the leaf, 'we'd have no talk
of an address of welcome' "—referring to an intended visit
of King Edward VII. In spite of his devotion to Parnell,
Hynes is regarded as a weakling, an inveterate sponger.

Henchy then comes in and alludes to the motif of
treachery and selling-out with the greeting, "No money,
boys." He begins to cast aspersions on Tierney's father
and, when Hynes departs, enacts his Judas-role, the easy-
going villain who desecrates the sacramental fire: "Mr.
Henchy snuffled vigorously and spat so copiously that he
nearly put out the fire, which uttered a hissing protest.
'To tell you my private and candid opinion,' he said.
'I think he's a man from the other camp. . . .' " Henchy's
coolness toward Hynes is indicated by his reserved nod
at him. His charge of Hynes's double-dealing and lack
of "manhood" seems proof that he is loyal to Tierney;
but what he is really obsessed with is compensation for
his services. Slight praise of Hynes's father and abomina-
tion of the son earns Old Jack's scornful condemnation
of Hynes. O'Connor's defense of Hynes mentions Hynes's
verses casually, but his effort to recall the verses as evidence
of Hynes's honesty is terminated by Henchy's outspoken
bigotry, illustrated by his opinion that the Fenians are
"in the pay of the Castle," ready to sell their country. At

this juncture, the ambiguous figure of Father Keon cuts in:

A person resembling a poor clergyman or a poor actor appeared in the doorway. His black clothes were tightly buttoned on his short body and it was impossible to say whether he wore a clergyman's collar or a layman's, because the collar of his shabby frock-coat, the uncovered buttons of which reflected the candlelight, was turned up about his neck. He wore a round hat of hard black felt. His face, shining with raindrops, had the appearance of damp yellow cheese save where two rosy spots indicated the cheekbones. He opened his very long mouth suddenly to express disappointment and at the same time opened wide his very bright blue eyes to express pleasure and surprise.

The duality compressed in the last sentence, juxtaposing disappointment and pleasure, is finally resolved in the "discreet, indulgent, velvety voice," asking for Mr. Fanning the money-lender. Afterwards Father Keon heads for the Black Eagle Tavern to consort with moneyed revelers. Henchy labels him a "black sheep," and his associations suggest the collusion of religious and secular elements in Irish politics. But this shabby clergyman, meddling in worldly affairs and neglecting spiritual duties, refuses to join the group of shiftless parasites. Nobody, however, can identify him or define his affiliation. His enigmatic role is formulated by O'Connor's questions: "What is he exactly? And how does he 'knock it out'?" Henchy places him whimsically but suggestively in the fabric of the plot: " 'God forgive me,' he says, 'I thought he was the dozen of stout" that he had requested earlier from Tierney. Henchy then pokes fun at the City Fathers and the Lord Mayor, joined in this ridicule by Old Jack.

With the new expectation for drink set up by Henchy, the interruption here by the boy with the bottles of stout is justified. Joyce's chief device, the miniature stage-play, presents a sequence of gestures (physical and verbal motions) enacted by personages who enter to deliver their parts and exit, engaging in conversations interrupted by the appearance and disappearance of other persons, the raking of cinders, corks popping. Political commentary is humorously counterpointed by a ground bass of small-minded bickering, booze, and mundane ado, frustrating the intrusion of lofty or "sublime" material. The narration may seem loosely held by impromptu questions and answers, improvised or chance remarks; but the development of the topics and their interweaving show thematic concentration on central motifs. The lulls and distracting moments, reflecting the unifying interests of the characters, seem deliberate: for example, after Henchy's smug censure of the patriot who would sell his country, a knock follows and our curiosity urges us to expect an affirmation or denial of Henchy's position. The canvassers unwittingly reveal their twisted minds in their talk while waiting for the benefactor's rewards. A dozen bottles of stout is the measure of their worth: the beer is both compensation and judgment. But thanks to their mean, gross sensibilities, triviality and drink make them cheerful.

The canvassers consider their employer an impudent and evasive fool, despising him as a "mean little schoolboy of hell"; they indulge in vehemently casting insults and calumny on their benefactor, even as Tierney himself dominates them as the object of their anxious waiting. When the stout arrives, Henchy, the chief turncoat, recants: "Ah, well, he's not so bad after all. He's as good as his word, anyhow. . . . He's not a bad sort, only Fanning has such a loan of him. He means well, you know, in his own tinpot way." This rationalizing compliment displays Henchy's moral depravity. He continues to express cynical distrust of his companions, criticizing Crofton: "He's not worth a damn as a canvasser."

Crofton and Lyons enter, with Lyons kidding Henchy

and O'Connor with severe, judicious indictment: "Is that the way you chaps canvass, and Crofton and I out in the cold and rain looking for votes?" Which, being true, provokes a spirited protest from Henchy. Lacking the corkscrew that the boy had brought—and youth, it seems, has the means to resolve the adult's problem—Henchy, who has accused Tierney of monopolizing tricks, demonstrates "his little trick" by placing the bottles on the hob. Waiting for the bottle to pop, Joyce supplies a description of Crofton. His physical appearance was broadly sketched when he entered the room ("a young ox's face"). His silence is explained: ". . . he had nothing to say; the second reason was that he considered his companions beneath him." Formerly a Conservative, Crofton has chosen "the lesser of two evils" (Tierney) as against the Nationalist Colgan who, to Hynes, represents the laboring class.

According to Lyons, Tierney "doesn't belong to any party, good, bad, or indifferent." He thus resembles Father Keon, whose identity has puzzled Henchy and O'Connor: in the formal context of the story, both Tierney and Father Keon function as coordinates in defining the inner selves of Hynes, Henchy, and all the other characters. Henchy doesn't object to the English monarch's visit, and when O'Connor demurs, he replies: "Parnell is dead." The apologetic "Pok" of the cork prepares Henchy's compromise, invoking fair play: "Let bygones be bygones." An enthusiastic dialogue foreshadows Hynes's return and his reading of his poem denouncing traitors. Amid the dispute about Parnell's "fortune" in life, the cautious O'Connor ventures to mediate:

> "This is Parnell's anniversary," said Mr. O'Connor, "and don't let us stir up any bad blood. We all respect him now that he's dead and gone—even the Conservatives," he added, turning to Mr. Crofton.
> Pok! The tardy cork flew out of Mr. Crofton's bottle. Mr.

Crofton got up from his box and went to the fire. As he
returned with his capture he said in a deep voice:
    "Our side of the house respects him, because he was a
gentleman."

Henchy's hedging conception of Parnell's statesmanship
reveals his view of the Irish wild beasts and Parnell as a
showy kind of circus tamer:

> "Right you are, Crofton!" said Mr. Henchy fiercely. He
> was the only man that could keep that bag of cats in order.
> "Down, ye dogs! Lie down, ye curs!" That's the way he
> treated them. "Come in, Joe! Come in!" he called out, catch-
> ing sight of Mr. Hynes in the doorway.

Henchy here plays the role of zealous coaxer and un-
abashed host and life of the party. He unwittingly goes
against his grain when he cancels his previous low estimation of Hynes: ". . . there's one of them, anyhow," said
Mr. Henchy, "that didn't renege him. By God, I'll say for
you, Joe! No, by God, you stuck to him like a man!"
Henchy and O'Connor persuade Henchy with blustering
tone to read his "splendid" verses.
    Hynes's elegiac homage, "The Death of Parnell," reflects
his character as naturally devoted to nationalistic ideals,
to the heroic past. The style of his poem is routine, with
stereotyped allegorical figures revolving around Parnell's
stature as a slain Caesar. The falling and rising movement
of the imagery, with death succeeded by resurrection,
establishes a symmetry of pattern that leads to the equation Parnell=Phoenix. Like Christ, Parnell has been betrayed by his partisans; however, Parnell will not rise again
in the body—nor, perhaps, in spirit. The grave decorum
of the poem exists in the satiric curse framed within a
hymn of mourning and vengeful triumph:

> May everlasting shame consume
> The memory of those who tried
> To befoul and smear the exalted name
> Of one who spurned them in his pride.

The succeeding two stanzas modulate into the statement of Parnell's heroic fall and a description of his calm repose in "peaks of glory," culminating with a prophetic paean which embodies the transcendent meaning of time comprehended in a mythical framework:

> They had their way: they laid him low.
> But Erin, list, his spirit may
> Rise, like the Phoenix from the flames,
> When breaks the dawning of the day,
>
> The day that brings us Freedom's reign.
> And on that day may Erin well
> Pledge in the cup she lifts to Joy
> One grief—the memory of Parnell.

The obvious irony is that Ivy Day shows us not "Freedom's reign" but selfish material interests ascendant; not a cup lifted to joy in memory of one grief but stout received as mere pittance. After the burst of clapping, the sound of "Pok" and the cork's flying out of Hynes's bottle mock by contrived accident the sentiments and serious tone of the poem. Hynes and the other listeners do not perceive the context of their excitement, being submerged in it. Hynes is portrayed as overwhelmed, "sitting flushed and bareheaded on the table." O'Connor tries to hide his emotions, while Henchy displays an uneasy feeling of guilt, taunting Crofton about the dubious merit of the poem. Only Crofton can sense the serious discrepancy between the lofty and bold feelings articulated by the poem, and the vulgar, shameful repudiation of those feelings by the people in the room. He properly adjusts his attitude to the circumstance and exercises restraint in his flat statement, significantly rendered by Joyce in indirect discourse: "Mr. Crofton said that it was a very fine piece of writing."

Hynes's verses, though artificially rhymed, nonetheless evoke fervent feelings and testify to the sincere intentions of the writer. The applause of this group, which has somehow betrayed their consciences, signifies not acceptance of, but mere acquiescence to, their base existence. Ivy Day finds these different menials in the committee room brought together less by common interest than by the chance of bad weather, and led spontaneously to an unplanned mock-celebration of Parnell's death anniversary. In the dismal, damp room, the canvassers fail to account for the darkness engulfing them, a darkness of their own making—the gloom of their paralyzed spirits. Parnell's spirit, evoked by the fire and the ivy leaves on their coats, discloses the corrupting malice and sloth of Ireland as represented by these men.

Ivy day, in effect, is dying out. Like Parnell, Tierney is betrayed by his chosen followers. To Henchy, Tierney represents irreverent youth usurping the reign of the old generation; such a transition does not augur progress or fulfillment but a helpless succumbing to the kind of life exemplified by the derelict Henchy. Henchy flaunts his knowing air and tries to prove his ingenuity by offering the bottles to the ebbing fire—again, an undercutting of the rite symbolized by the interlocking images of leaf-fire-brew-candles. Will the momentary feelings of the ward-heeler lead to an awakening, a recognition of his impotence and his fellows' collective need of regeneration? Parnell's memory has induced only a release of tears, an impasse (pathos) whereby characters emerge absolutely defined in their doomed state.

Detached and feeling superior, Crofton is the only char-

acter slightly aware of a situation marked by party fac-
tionalism and its overthrowing of ideals and principles.
He respects Parnell in spite of the moral liability attached
to him by orthodox Ireland; the other canvassers praise
but dishonor Parnell in their deceitful behavior. With
singleminded purpose, Parnell brought a fleeting glory
to the decaying old order; the flicker of remembrance,
imaged by the feeble fire, helps uncork the bottles. The
three poks, echoing a funeral salute, undercut the declared
thoughts and sentiments of the men; their apologetic
sound suggests the superficial ceremony that marks the
unintended vigil of the canvassers. In the spooky atmosphere, what is celebrated is not any single historical actor;
rather, it is the death of principle. Jealousies, backbiting,
and blarney replace ritual as tribute to the twin deities
of drink and money. Crofton seems to be the disguised
power of darkness as he perceives from a distance the in-
fidelity and venal sinfulness of everyone. He preserves a
reserved, tolerant silence, realizing Parnell's greatness in
the face of present degeneration.

The ivy motif, a symbol of the creative matrix of nature,
combines the themes of pride and the salvation of dead
souls. The images of ivy leaf, fire, stout, and so on convey
ambivalent meanings that confirm the link between appearance and reality. Spiritual poverty and alienation
find correlatives in objective phenomena. Cinder, flames,
smoke, and bottles on the hob constitute the paltry para-
phernalia for the travesty of the thanksgiving rite. The
doggerel elevates fire to iconic importance by alluding to
Parnell as a Phoenix rising from the flames—a miracle
postulated on the acknowledgment of mutual dependence
between the living and the dead. Cork and leaf comment
on each other; ivy leaf, sacred to Dionysus, suggests intoxi-
cation that exercises power over men crowding near the
dying hearthfire. Ivy Day sanctifies Bacchus, not Parnell.
The men are dead, but Parnell, though literally dead, rises

from the past as living rebuke. Salvation in drink promises temporary reprieve. The background of the past, like the environment, dominates over the foreground, the present occurrence. The sober sense of a need for commitment aroused by the poem attests partly to a hidden resource for renewal in the responsive characters. But given the permanent traits of these men, such as Henchy's holier-than-thou attitude and the inertia afflicting O'Connor, it is difficult to conceive of an immediate turnabout in their lives. With the drinking habit—"the thin edge of the wedge"—ingrained in youth (the delivery boy, for example), and reverence for the aged no longer shown, it is difficult to expect a quick cultivation of self-discipline and moral integrity. Sickly Old Jack, lighting two candles, functions as the herald of death and patron of the burial rite. With the men's moral fiber possessed by malignant disease, the future seems to hold no promise.

Ivy leaf and phoenix fire, emblems of regeneration, orient the vivid Daumier-like portrayals of these canvassers, pointing up the antithesis between remembered past glory and present tawdry circumstances. If mean expedience denies possible regeneration, then the commemoration of the death of rectitude is warranted. The action of the story has successfully harmonized professed intentions and inner motives in a convergence of time and place focused in a single occasion attuned to a predominant elegiac-ironic mood. Lacking any change of setting, Joyce's story seems to locate the evil of paralysis and atrophied will in the unredeemable fatality—the superintending *genius loci*—which informs the lives of the characters.

Joyce's objective method of presentation allows for a varied irony resulting from sustained contrasts between great and small, between the niggardly and ineffectual lives of the men and Parnell's noble calling. The effect of incongruity, elaborately developed by tactful accumulation of details, may strike one as a bad stylistic joke, a comic paradox. And the doubleness of meaning inherent in Joyce's narrative method may not completely justify a melodramatic reversal in the movement from sudden elevation of mood (as during the reading of the poem) and abrupt descent into bathos (the reverse of pathos). Joyce's vision, however, is premised on a lucid critical awareness arising from the constant clash of attitude and conduct. The cork's popping may be interpreted as a device for transposing the stature of the characters from the fraudulently righteous to the blatantly vulgar. The slightly mawkish but genuine response of the canvassers to Hynes's declamation reduces the distance of the reader from the sordid, low humor characteristic of the men. The discerning reader who experiences this dual attitude of being sympathetically moved and detached at the same time—the precise effect of Joyce's craft—finds himself in a favorable condition to appreciate the complex juxtaposition of negation and affirmation of which "Ivy Day in the Committee Room" is the heightened representation.

13
A MOTHER

WHEREAS IN "THE BOARDING HOUSE," THE FIGURE OF MRS.
Mooney as "The Madam" incorporates the narrator's hind-
sight and foresight, in this story Joyce moves a little distance away from his protagonist, Mrs. Kearney, placing her
in a concourse of incidents that produce a change in her
fortune by reiterating a habitual choice. One can grasp
the story's principle of composition by observing how the
ironic complications revolve around one principal episode—the concerts sponsored by the *Eire Abu* society. The
mother, Mrs. Kearney, wants to exercise her motherhood
on a social affair, disrupting others' plans and setting up
her own conditions to satisfy her inner motives. Joyce
exhibits for critical scrutiny the outcome of the action
hinging on the change in the protagonist's thought.

Less pictorial description than scenic presentation, "A
Mother" displays a plot which exhibits an action centering
on a change of a kind that reveals the protagonist's moral
character as she moves from one situation to another. For
the purpose of analysis, we may divide the story into three
parts. The first part formulates the precipitating cause
that brings the protagonist to the first state. It shows us
Mrs. Kearney wresting the initiative from the male (rep-

resented by Holohan, the assistant secretary of the *Eire Abu*). After this summary report conveyed in the opening paragraph, Joyce then explains how Mrs. Kearney succeeded in "arranging everything" because she is the kind of person who can conceive means to promote her own interests, and incidentally her daughter's. The conflict of self and circumstance elaborated in the dramatized episodes of the story begins with Mrs. Kearney's personal life-history before she became a mother. We find in her background the causes of her disconcerting behavior and attitudes that unfold ironically, during the concert:

> Miss Devlin had become Mrs. Kearney out of spite. She had been educated in a high-class convent where she had learned French and music. As she was naturally pale and unbending in manner she made few friends at school. When she came to the age of marriage she was sent out to many houses where her playing and ivory manners were much admired. She sat amid the chilly circle of her accomplishments, waiting for some suitor to brave it and offer her a brilliant life. But the young men whom she met were ordinary and she gave them no encouragement, trying to console her romantic desires by eating a great deal of Turkish delight in secret. However, when she drew near the limit and her friends began to loosen their tongues about her she silenced them by marrying Mr. Kearney, who was a bootmaker on Ormond Quay.

The telling phrases—"naturally pale and unbending," "ivory manners," "romantic desires"—also contain the basis for a counterplot action which is first hinted at in Holohan's shifty conduct. With her "ivory manners" and her indulgence in Turkish delight, Mrs. Kearney combines shrewd practicality with a puritanical earnestness. Accordingly, she marries a docile bootmaker, pious and respectable as the Post Office—precisely the antithesis of the romantic lover she had envisioned for herself. But, it must be emphasized here, "she never put her own romantic ideas away."

Mrs. Kearney has never renounced her feminine self: she acknowledges the abstract value of the husband as male, though imposing her will on him. The male species —like Holohan and his ilk—is only a means to her ends. Overcome by the wife, his initiative paralyzed, the meek bootmaker submits to an existence that other husbands would endure only with resentment or indifference. With the animus in her psyche toward males subdued, Mrs. Kearney assumes the authority of the male. She begins to use her daughter as a medium to realize her thwarted ambitions in a vicarious way. But just as her strong will helped her become a mother, it also dooms her as a mother. Given her inborn traits and background, Mrs. Kearney subscribes to a code embodying a perverted ideal of legality that resists adjustment to changing conditions and fights any compromise with necessity—the actual forces at work in life. Both her husband and daughter obey Mrs. Kearney's wishes; nothing in her family life, in her role as mother, warns her of the drawback or danger of maintaining an "unbending" stance before the uncontrolled flow of events.

Events in the story demonstrate the serious pathos of Mrs. Kearney's situation. She wagers her personal fortune against an environment which she knows will never yield to her own urgent desires. She manifests her own incorrigible fixation on an ideal of success that will make excessive demands on the inadequate material of experience. Her blind conformity to her own schemes makes her forget that her own success has so far been confined to the choice of husband and the management of her domestic life.

From the start Mrs. Kearney's struggle against isolation leads to her unbalanced marriage. Her pious motherly concern for her daughter, abetted by a current of vindictiveness against anti-romantic life, drives her to take advantage

of the Irish revival, the nationalistic sentiment manifested
in postcards and cultural affairs. Circumstances seem pro-
pitious for fulfilling her dreams, this time through her
daughter, Kathleen. Her motherhood gives her an opportunity to mediate between grandiose, inordinate ambition
and mediocre surroundings.

Thus we find Mrs. Kearney seizing Holohan's proposal.
Note that it was the man who approached the woman:
"She entered heart and soul into the details of the enterprise, advised and dissuaded" until a contract was drawn
up. Hopping with his game leg, Holohan proved absolutely
inefficient, so that in the end Mrs. Kearney "arranged
everything." But her tact and delicate sense of arranging
the program did not take contingencies into account (for
example, *artistes* like Madame Glynn) , especially the false
enthusiasm of the Committee and the boorish, easily dis-
gruntled audience. The narrator's comment delivers a
finely edged irony: "She forgot nothing and, thanks to her,
everything that was to be done was done."

The second part of the story consists of the beginning
of the concert on Wednesday night, climaxed with the
moment when Mrs. Kearney learns that the Friday concert is to be canceled. She immediately buttonholes the
limping busybody, Holohan: "—But, of course, that doesn't
alter the contract, she said." Coarse, insensible forces now
mass against Mrs. Kearney. Holohan earns proper con-
tempt for his unmanly evasiveness. He shifts the responsibility to the secretary, Mr. Fitzpatrick. Her unfavorable
impression of the secretary, with his vacant face and hat
askew, chewing one end of the program into a moist pulp
and seeming to bear disappointments lightly, should have
cautioned her. But her rigid frame of mind and her
temperamental outbursts defeat her intentions in the end.

Meanwhile, however, Mrs. Kearney suppresses her
anger: "But she knew that it would not be ladylike to do
that: so she was silent." This notion suffers a reversal in

the end. Her "ivory manners," polished but rigid, prove
ascendant in restraining her impulsive masculinity. Besides, her husband's presence allays her suspicions and
reassures her. But although she appreciated her husband's
"abstract value as a male," the fact is that her notion remains abstract. The role of the sexes reversed by her
usurping the husband's prerogative, Mrs. Kearney forfeits
the male's assistance and antagonizes the ineffectual men
of the Committee. Her habit of adhering to her plans
forces her to demand from the Committee immediate
payment according to the contract. She insists before the
noncommittal Holohan: "I have my contract and I mean
to see it."

Holohan's figure sums up the chaotic, futile response of
the crowd and the increasing alienation among Mrs.
Kearney, the performers, and the Committee. When the
contract yields to circumstance, we see how life itself can
frustrate human designs. The omission of the Friday concert in favor of a Saturday gala night (which never ma-
terializes) because of the poor response to the Wednesday
and Thursday performances could not have been foreseen
until it actually happened. Everything—time, place, milieu
—seems to conspire against Mrs. Kearney's virtuous independence, mocking her tradition-bound respect for contracts. She protests against the Committee, not against life,
accusing it of cheating her.

To make Mrs. Kearney's situation less hopeful of gratifying success, Joyce introduces in the middle of the narrative,
right after Holohan has in cowardly fashion parried the
irate mother's thrust, two figures, the dapper *Freeman*
reporter and O'Madden Burke. These two "had taken
possession of the fireplace." The *Freeman* man's description—"plausible voice," "careful manners," and aroma of
cigar—easily places him as a romantic type. The narrative
style adjusts itself to support that dreamy facet of Mrs.
Kearney's personality which sustains her unyielding hon-

esty. Talking to Miss Healey, the *Freeman* man "was pleasantly conscious that the bosom which he saw rise and fall slowly beneath him rose and fell at that moment for him, that the laughter and fragrance and wilful glances were his tribute." The reporter's egotism parodies Mrs. Kearney's self-centered interest in the concert.

On the other hand, the "gentleman," O'Madden Burke, lends support to the pragmatic and expedient talent of Mrs. Kearney. Notice the blunt sardonic tone and irony of Joyce's portrait: "He was a suave elderly man who balanced his imposing body, when at rest, upon a large silk umbrella. His magniloquent western name was the moral umbrella upon which he balanced the fine problem of his finances. He was widely respected." Juxtaposed with the hypocritical and morally defective society epitomized by O'Madden Burke, Mrs. Kearney's "unlady-like" attack and withdrawal in the end seem just, the more so when it is men like Holohan and O'Madden Burke who offer judgment: "You did the proper thing, Holohan, said Mr. O'Madden Burke, poised upon his umbrella in approval." ("Umbrella" draws on both the physical and figurative usages in the early description.) While Holohan's limp betrays his irresponsible nature, O'Madden Burke's portrait (as Joyce renders it) repudiates his pretense of infallible judgment.

It is difficult to side with unfeeling and ineffectual men like Holohan and O'Madden Burke. On the other hand, though Mrs. Kearney's situation attracts our sympathy, the narrative calls attention to her unlikable qualities; deficient in feminine grace, she turns out to be not a warm, tolerant mother, but a cold, calculating woman whose self-righteous indignation makes her a victim of circumstance. She craves success for her daughter, but later seems determined to exact any sacrifice to obtain monetary compensation. What she envisages as the attainment of her goal (the solid cash of eight guineas) seems not to recompense her loss of restraint and dignity. The Committee accedes to paying half of the contract. Upon that offer of merely a token payment (her business acumen, not her romantic predilection controls her now), Mrs. Kearney reveals the measure of her personality as a failed dreamer and, in social occasions, a crude, money-minded boss. When the reality proves to be outside the range of her plans, she loses her composure. Her hopes gradually dissolve amid the rabble's hootings, and this aggrieved mother congeals into "an angry stone image."

Following the Committee's threat not to honor the contract if Kathleen does not play in the second part, the heated exchange between Holohan and Mrs. Kearney shows us the reversal of the mother's solicitous image in the drawing room, with her decanter and silver biscuit barrel, nicely accommodating. Observe now the mother's proud wrongheaded posture, her fanatical devotion to the letter of the contract:

—I haven't seen any Committee, said Mrs. Kearney angrily. My daughter has her contract. She will get four pounds eight into her hand or a foot she won't put on that platform. . . .

Her face was inundated with an angry colour and she looked as if she would attack someone with her hands.

—I'm asking for my rights, she said.

—You might have some sense of decency, said Mr. Holohan.

—Might I, indeed? . . . And when I ask when my daughter is going to be paid I can't get a civil answer.

She tossed her head and assumed a haughty voice:

—You might speak to the secretary. It's not my business. I'm a great fellow fol-the-diddle-I-do.

—I thought you were a lady, said Mr. Holohan, walking away from her abruptly.

After that Mrs. Kearney's conduct was condemned on all hands. . . .

Earlier, the *artistes* were noncommittal, interested only in money. But appearances mislead: the second tenor "covered his nervous jealousy with an ebullient friendliness." The mother's increasing isolation worsens when she appeals to Miss Healey, who, at first feigning sympathy, later abandons the mother and complies with the Committee's request. Holohan would not have been surprised if he had known of Mrs. Kearney's past, which the narrator summarizes in the second and third paragraphs of the story. Her situation in a sense calls forth such attitudes of defiant insistence and massive stubbornness, which are the inevitable outcome of her character moving through the situations contrived, at first, by her, then slowly manipulated and directed by the Committee and the audience— the whole Dublin milieu. Her sense of being wronged, aggravated by the insensitive Committee, occasions her aggressive spite and offsets all possibility of concession on her part. With a fixed mind, refusing all compromise, she looms a formidable figure haughtily superior to her disappointment, making up for the loss she "earns" in the end by not modifying her insistent adherence to contracts.

We see that all the facts about Mrs. Kearney converge in her dominating attitude, her romantic flair degenerating into obsessive concern with her daughter's payment. Her conduct is logically consistent. The emotional effect of her actions, however, is modified by her shift from large romantic hopes to legalism and finally to covetous interest in cash. In effect, she violates an unwritten code then prevailing that musical contracts, improvised and contingent on daily results, are more promising than binding. Mrs. Kearney loses her sense of proportion, making of a discomfiture a question of honor and trust. She creates a break in the transaction between her family and Dublin society, freeing herself from the obligation of adapting her thoughts to the limitations of her surroundings. What she had arranged, reality violated and wrecked.

The reader would be more antagonistic to Mrs.

Kearney's behavior if the *artistes* had not manifested crude affectations and other distasteful qualities. On the whole, they cancel our unqualified approval: Mr. Bell is jealous of other tenors; the thoughtless Mr. Duggan wipes his nose with his glove; the first tenor and the baritone exude an alienating "opulence." Just as the concert numbers were assembled without any taste, so the participants were expediently gathered without any standard of excellence to govern their selection. This corresponds with the audience's fake interest in culture. The Committee's notion of the concert as a box office affair converts the whole scene in the concert room to a miniature hell, displaying a variety of petty vices. Joyce manages the scenes of the story so that they implicitly criticize the propriety of Mrs. Kearney's behavior, with the moral worth of her character determining our emotional responses to her actions. Curiously enough, her dutiful legalism appears to be sanctioned by the mores of her society.

While Mrs. Kearney displays a self-assertive personality governed by the idea of success, Miss Beirne presents a counter-image, intimating the complete turnabout in Mrs. Kearney's attitude to Holohan. With oldish face "screwed into an expression of trustfulness and enthusiasm," Miss Beirne's appearance signals a gradual discounting of Mrs. Kearney's expectations: Miss Beirne "looked out at the rain until the melancholy of the wet street effaced all the trustfulness and enthusiasm from her twisted features." While Miss Beirne parodies the unctuous or conscientious gravity of Mrs. Kearney, the effaced Madame Glynn heightens the pathos of the unavailing past. Madame Glynn's "has-been" features and her pale face and faded dress, suggest the slow decay of polite manners and culture in Ireland. She fails to revive sentiment for the old Irish ballad with her antiquated style: "The poor lady sang *Killarney* in a bodiless gasping voice, with all the old-fashioned mannerisms of intonation and pronunciation which she believed lent elegance to her singing. She looked as if she had been resurrected from an old stage-wardrobe and the cheaper parts of the hall made fun of her high-wailing notes." In contrast to this shabby relic of old opera, Mrs. Kearney, a strong-willed matriarch with an outraged conscience, affirms, not the elegant refinement of the Irish romantic past, but its obstinate, rebellious instinct for survival. While the *Freeman* reporter cancels the genteel aspect of courtly love, Madame Glynn cancels the power of genteel life to remedy the loss of ordinary human affections, and the cynical indifference of most Dubliners.

Recognizing all the limitations of the story's anti-heroic protagonist and her inability to transcend her circumscribed knowledge because of an innate rigidity, we refrain from totally condemning Mrs. Kearney. Our attention is deflected to the censure of Holohan and O'Madden Burke as persons not to be depended upon for a fair verdict. The final impression we get is also influenced by the revelation of the conflict in the protagonist between her desires and the resistance of her environment, with the plot amplifying the discrepancies between her uncompromising attitude and the recalcitrant fatality of her position. We perceive how Mrs. Kearney's predicament follows from her nature; we admire her determination to pursue her plans, yet reserve our outright disapproval when she refuses to profit from the lessons of experience. Mrs. Kearney's defeat in this episode, precipitated by the negative response of Dublin to the concert, actualizes and reiterates the given potentialities of her character. We feel superior to her in surveying the whole, and while we feel that what happened to Mrs. Kearney is unjust and slightly undeserved in the light of her efforts to help the Committee, yet we do not admire her desperate covetousness. All Dublin becomes an accomplice in Mrs. Kearney's failure. This primary caustic effect, which stimulates profound uneasiness in the reader who customarily seeks a neat resolution for the hero and the villain, makes "A Mother" the best representative of the type of stories in *Dubliners*.

14
GRACE

ORIGINALLY THE CONCLUDING STORY OF *Dubliners,* "GRACE" has not received the formal elucidation it deserves mainly because of the misleading approach critics have used, distracting us from the proper inquiry into the intrinsic causes of our pleasure in reading it. We learn from Stanislaus Joyce's biography that Joyce planned the story with the pattern of Dante's *Divine Comedy* in mind: "Mr. Kernan's fall down the steps of the lavatory is his descent into hell, the sickroom is purgatory, and the Church in which he and his friends listen to the sermon is paradise at last." Are Father Purdon and his temporizing materialism Joyce's image of Paradise? To sacrifice the irony of the story for the sake of superimposing an abstract scheme is to reduce our complex emotional response into one-dimensional concepts. Consequently, most explications of "Grace" forfeit their relevance to our experience. For they assume the report to be equivalent to the meaning of the story and simply draw up a foregone conclusion, forcing even literal and straightforward details into symbolic straitjackets. To prove that Joyce had planned the story in terms of a threefold division does not explain how the story acquires unity, or how the formal wholeness of the parts affords the unique pleasure and insight we get from reading it.

The plot of "Grace" is composed of three episodes, the first two of which produce an effect by unfolding a basic defect in the protagonist's character, diminishing the sympathy we feel toward him and giving us a sense of superiority over him without completely satisfying our demand for justice. The last episode is nonpainful, enhancing our detachment by the narrative mode of distancing the protagonist's fate and its pathetic implications. By concentrating on Father Purdon's sermon at the end, Joyce clarifies the nature of Kernan's choice and reiterates its distinctive character, stressing the protagonist's inability to perceive the moral consequences of his choice.

It is a common habit to interpret the opening incident—Kernan's fall in the lavatory, which renders him unconscious and therefore puts him at the mercy of others—as reflecting the condition of man as fallen creature. The function of this scene, in terms of illustrating the character's initial situation before the change begins to take place, is mainly expository. It prepares for the decisive stage, Kernan's assent to his friend's "plot." Uninformed as yet of his attitudes, tastes, and opinions, we naturally sympathize with an injured man smeared with filth, lying face downward.

Nobody can identify the customer. Alarmed by the man's "grey pallor," the manager of the pub sends for a constable. Suspicious, "as if he feared to be the victim of some delusion" (in contrast to the trusting Kernan), the constable proceeds to inquire about the man's identity. Kernan's incognito correlates later with his lack of self-knowledge, which lack we infer from the action of the story.

Everyone is helpless until an unknown young man in a cycling suit arrives and restores consciousness to Kernan. We look down upon the manager, the inert spectators, and even the constable who represents impersonal authority—all seem impotent to give aid or to resolve the emergency, as if each had participated in the fall.

One revealing trait of the protagonist is indicated by his habit at the start either of understating the seriousness of his physical hurt or of shamefacedly concealing the pain he is suffering. Ignoring the constable's queries, Kernan "made light of the accident." Ironically, he obscures the nature of his suffering. We see that he is not a man given to self-pity or to exaggerating his personal condition in order to be the object of charity. On the other hand, he is not ungrateful: he thanks the mysterious young man thrice. "The shock and the incipient pain had partly sobered him." The narrative action shows that while Kernan slowly awakens to the truth of his physical condition, he never even begins to recognize the truth of his own spiritual or moral condition.

One other function of the opening incident, apart from demonstrating the dominant trait of the protagonist that will condition his choice later, is the introduction of Power. The encaging ring of onlookers represents the anonymous collective that demands enlightenment as to the cause of the catastrophe, not the deplorable state of the injured man. It takes an unknown young man to revive Kernan, while an old friend like Power (see the references to Power in Mrs. Kernan's reminiscence) holds back until he is assured that Kernan is physically sound. He fears being implicated in a scandalous accident.

Joyce then dramatizes in the car scene the relation between Power and Kernan. In transit Power, with a matchflame no bigger than the speck of red light at the Jesuit Church, discovers that Kernan has bitten off a piece of his tongue. Again, to Power's remark ("That's ugly"), Kernan responds with self-effacing nonchalance, more striking since his profession as teataster will be seriously affected by his injury. Since the protagonist does not really suffer, our pity loses support. We observe his relative superiority to Power, a man with "inexplicable debts."

Before we are introduced to Mrs. Kernan, we are given a summary presentation of Kernan's mania for fashionable clothes, for "his silk hat of some decency," by grace of which "a man could always pass muster." He believed in the dignity of his calling, but "modern business methods" have precipitated his decline—although friends of his successful past "still esteem him as a character." This account of his background, interposed between the initial event and the visit of his friends, prepares us for the kind of reception and accommodation he gives them.

The conversation between Mrs. Kernan and Power detracts from our good impression of Kernan. We learn that he has spent his money on drink, and has been abandoned by Harford and his dissipated cronies, who turn out later to be members of the "body" in the retreat. The wife's complaints seem confirmed by the children's horseplay. Power's apologetic tone (with his "inexplicable debts" foreshadowing the moral bookkeeping of Father Purdon) prepares us for his announcement of a mission to reconvert Kernan, to "make a new man of him." Martin Cunningham serves as the good shepherd to bring Kernan back to the fold.

So far, our conception of Kernan's character has been unfavorably modified by his wife's testimony. How fair is she in appraising her errant husband, in judging the depth of his disgrace? The narrative directly supplies us with information on the basis of which we can formulate our estimate of her role in relation to the development of the change in Kernan, a change that simply brings out a dominant tendency in his mechanism of choice. Kernan appears to be in a bad fix. His wife, although an active and practical woman, is really a dreamy sentimentalist charmed by romantic weddings. But within three

weeks of her own wedding "she had found a wife's life
irksome and unbearable, until she became a mother."
Thenceforth she has efficiently administered her household, for which she is to be credited. Although she scolds
her husband for intemperance, she also tolerates it as "a
part of the climate." In part we may say that she is
responsible for Kernan's "fall" in the lavatory. Kernan's
wife merits no pity because of her incapacity to see what
is wrong with herself and her refusal to contrive a permanent solution for what clearly remains a potential
source of suffering—her husband's drinking, her ineffectual exhortation. Kernan himself is indifferent to the harm
he does himself and his family, and is blind to his own
misfortune.

We learn that Mrs. Kernan also needs a moral turnover.
She resents her husband's sharp tongue and secretly re-
joices over his accident:

> Religion for her was a habit and she suspected that a man
> of her husband's age would not change greatly before death.
> She was tempted to see a curious appropriateness in his acci-
> dent and, but that she did not wish to seem bloody-minded,
> she would have told the gentlemen that Mr. Kernan's tongue
> would not suffer by being shortened.

Though she is not sensitive enough to admit her part in
her own discomfiture, she is discreet and decorous in her
performance of her duties, especially before visitors. Later
Mrs. Kernan will wisely conceal her satisfaction at the
success of his friends. Our impression of her, however,
has taken a negative coloring which makes us assume a
superior viewpoint. She is important to the plot, obviously,
because she provides the cause for Kernan's assent to his
friends' plan, assent which displays the characteristic *ethos*
motivating his decisions in life.

Before that incident, however, the narrative has furnished us the facts that make Kernan's reputed change (to repeat, the change is superficial and what the plot demonstrates is a reiterated choice) both surprising and inevitable. The narrative stresses that Kernan's bedroom is "impregnated with a personal odour," and his attitude suggests how he will respond to his guests: "He apologized to his guests for the disorder of the room but at the same time looked at them a little proudly, with a veteran's pride." We are also told that Kernan was "quite unconscious that he was the victim of a plot." This means that he would be returned to the pale of the Church from which he had presumably wandered for twenty years, assuming that the Church opposes the worldliness practised by Kernan. We discover later that the retreat at the Jesuit church simply guarantees the permanence of Kernan's ways.

At first, the plot seems to generate the reformation of an erring man, which would then satisfy the reader's desire for punitive correction, seeing that Kernan has been negligent of his duties as husband and father. But what is curiously ironic here is the idea of morality the friends entertain. Reacting to Kernan's defective nature, the reader hopes that Cunningham's plot will succeed—until he is shocked to find out at the end that it is not a conversion at all but an affirmation that Kernan's present ways will be preserved, if not worsened, by the sanction of Scriptures and the example of the Church.

Our response to Kernan's pseudo-change—his decision to make the retreat—which turns out to be a disguised reiteration of a habitual choice not to modify his present ways (in fact, to be assured of pious insurance for his errors), depends also on our appraisal of the "conspirators." It appears that all are in debt, suffering degrees of "disgrace." Material debt coalesces with spiritual sinfulness in Father Purdon's sermon; the difference between them disappears, and all present seem to be liable to

forfeiture of their trustworthy names. The sensible, in-
fluential, and intelligent-looking Cunningham "had
married an unpresentable woman who was an incurable
drunkard" and pawned his furniture periodically. Out-
witted by his derelict wife, the astute Cunningham is able
to persuade the obstinate Kernan to join the company in
a retreat. That piece of information completely destroys
the impression of Cunningham as a capable man (see Mrs.
Kernan's false opinion) who will staunchly execute the
project of making Kernan "wash the pot." His deceptive
face resembles those of the social *personae* of his friends
in masking the wretched anarchy of their private lives.

Despite their thriving occupations, Kernan's friends are
failures. The two paragraphs devoted to Cunningham's life
compose an ironical exposure of his personality. M'Coy,
the failed tenor, has always lived by his sly wits, shifting
from job to job. His manner of living makes his claim
to reliability precarious and open to doubt. Among the
plotters there exist grave disparities and hidden animosi-
ties. While Cunningham claims to be a judge of character
and an authority on all subjects, M'Coy plays the role of
odd dissenter: he praises Father Burke for preaching un-
orthodox ideas. He is timid, but impertinent. On the other
hand, Fogarty has earlier failed in business, but his in-
gratiating manners signal an optimistic development of
Power's scheme when he enters in the middle of the central
episode.

The conversation itself, neatly divided into two parts by
Fogarty's entrance, is punctuated with petty talk, inanities,
jokes, and drinking, mingling superficial camaraderie and
deep-rooted antipathies. The particular utterances of the
characters illustrate the generalized descriptions of the sum-
marized dossiers on Kernan's friends. Numerous scholars
have pointed out the misquotations, twisted facts, and
other burlesque mistakes committed by Cunningham, the

prime offender. and his friends, mistakes that ridicule their
solemn pertinacity and debunk their pretense to the lofty
and sacred. Such profane lapses surely alienate all sympathy from this group. What needs clarification is the way
the faults and defects of the "plotters" minimize Kernan's
deficiency in self-knowledge. At the beginning of the exchange, Kernan shows his singleminded, independent
frame of mind. He dismisses Cunningham and M'Coy,
but expresses gratitude to Power. Disclosure of Harford
as Kernan's drinking companion threatens for a while to
disrupt the smooth progression of the scheme, but Power
helps Kernan to change the subject, only to make Kernan
indignant: "The narrative made Mr. Kernan indignant.
He was keenly conscious of his citizenship, wished to live
with his city on terms mutually honorable and resented
any affront put upon him by those whom he called country
bumpkins." This disposition, above all other factors,
motivates Kernan's joining the retreat suggested by his
friends.

Cunningham's amusing anecdote fails to relax Kernan's
somewhat exaggerated indignation. But he is pacified by
Cunningham's diplomatic comment that the world is inhabited by some good and some bad people. Bantering
exchange between Kernan and his wife purges all irritants
and restores harmony. The next phase of the talk leads
to Cunningham's confession of their "plot." Taken into
his friends' confidence and given the honor of being invited to participate in the retreat, "Mr. Kernan was silent.
The proposal conveyed very little meaning to his mind
but, understanding that some spiritual agencies were about
to concern themselves on his behalf, he thought he owed
it to his dignity to show a stiff neck." Kernan's prudence,
based on a dubious notion of dignity, enables him to
maintain his "calm enmity." He approves of the Jesuits
because they "cater for the upper classes" and agrees with

the consensus that the Jesuits are all good men. Kernan
reiterates his high opinion of Cunningham as a judge of
character and as a reader of faces.

M'Coy interrupts with the name of Father Tom Burke,
leading to Kernan's recall of his friendship with the Prot-
estant Crofton. Kernan moves away again from Cunningham's position. He believes, with Crofton, that Protestants
and Catholics subscribe to the same belief—a jarring note
in the conversation but totally in accord with Kernan's
skeptical disposition. Cunningham's power over Kernan
has been established earlier and is reaffirmed when Kernan
warmly agrees with Cunningham's assertion that "our religion is *the* religion, the old original faith." Kernan seems
most affected by the force of "our." This tendency in
Kernan to be at peace with his city, reinforced by
Fogarty's gift of whiskey, persuades him to abide by
Cunningham's wisdom.

In the second part of the conversation, which deals
largely with the issue of Papal infallibility, Kernan
broaches the subject of immoral Popes and again menaces
the mutual understanding attained by the group. But
Cunningham skillfully diverts the talk to the infallibility
of the Pope. Under the influence of whiskey, all grow
solemn, thrilled by the "deep raucous voice" which utters
the word of belief and submission: "Credo." After uttering admiration for John MacHale, the bishop who at first
objected to the dogma of infallibility but later retracted
(a prefiguration of Kernan's attitude to his friends'
scheme) , Kernan seems finally convinced, unresisting, and
pliable as Power concludes the proceedings:

—Well, Mrs. Kernan, we're going to make your man here a
good holy pious and God-fearing Roman Catholic. He swept
his arm round the company inclusively.
—We're all going to make a retreat together and confess our
sins—and God knows we want it badly.

—I don't mind, said Mr. Kernan, smiling a little nervously.

So far Kernan has not shown himself mean or contemptible in any marked sense. He has not proved a
foolish disbeliever; he can not appreciate the good intentions of his friends, although his understanding of Cunningham's character (all his friends are morally suspect)
imposes a definite limit on his choice. His "little tale
of woe" may be designed to renounce the devil, but to
renounce him without "forgetting his works and pomps,"
as Cunningham proclaims, with felicitous *double entendre*
in the light of Father Purdon's compromise with Mammon.

Cunningham's exclamation is a significant clue to the
betrayal of any sincere impulse Kernan may cherish in
his breast. Yet, even at the close of this episode, Kernan
proves himself a sturdy loner equipped with an obdurate
mind, damning the candle business with "farcical gravity."
His protesting wish to bar "the magic-lantern business"
stimulates hearty laughter, depriving the situation of any
painful element of constraint while at the same time
depriving it also of any serious evidence that the retreat
will contribute to Kernan's enlightenment.

The painful sensation that Kernan felt in the lavatory
restored his consciousness; but here, throughout the exchange between Kernan and the "plotters," nothing generates self-awareness or prods his passive consciousness into
a genuine desire to reform himself. When the narrative
moves to the next episode, we watch how the retreat
affords a setting for Kernan's spurious "conversion." But
whatever punitive urge we have to correct the absurdities
of the five characters is discharged on Father Purdon
and sublimated to intellectual curiosity.

The narrative closing throws its emphasis, not on the
protagonist's weakness and his self-imposed deception, but
rather on Father Purdon and his distorted construing of

the Biblical text. For the source of any dissatisfaction we may have about Kernan and his friends can really be attributed to Father Purdon and his persuasive hold on the audience composed of worldly businessmen, both the successful and the failures, including Harford, the cowardly companion who deserted Kernan in his calamitous fall down the lavatory steps. Noting all these respectable members of the congregation, Kernan "began to feel more at home," with his "rehabilitated hat" placed in security. We can infer from earlier descriptions (Kernan "had never been seen in the city without a silk hat of some decency"; during his wedding, he carried "a silk hat gracefully balanced") that the hat possesses a universalizing quality as a sign of respectable status. Dirtied and battered by Kernan's fall, the hat makes him a nameless outcast. After temporarily losing balance and damaging his hat, Kernan is reinstated in society.

So far, we have inferred from the dramatic portrayal of Kernan's friends in dialogue how all of them need "grace" to rectify their lives. Our feelings for them, however, recoil before the display of their conceited minds and petty vanities. It is true that, gifted with a sense of humor, delicacy, and restraint, they (Power and Cunningham in particular) do not force Kernan to accept what to them appears as a good thing. They try to persuade him to approve of the retreat, to cooperate with the group. For without inner consent on his part, the efficacy of the retreat will be undermined; no amount of external imposition will make Kernan a new man. But the retreat turns out to be a force that will preserve and even strengthen the old Adam in Kernan and his friends.

In the central episode in Kernan's bedroom, we detect in the conversation a mock-serious and facetious undertone that prevents us from being really assured that Kernan will achieve a recognition of his defects or shortcomings. Given the solidarity of the businessmen and Kernan's belief in the "dignity of his calling," there is a great probability that Kernan will recover materially. His sharp tongue and his disaffection with the Church seem to have contributed to his commercial decline. During the latter part of the conversation, Kernan's independence of judgment seems corroded by liquor; his own estimate of his friends, we know, rests on ignorance. Nonetheless, we refrain from completely despising him for subverting his frank "veteran's pride" in pleasing others, for submerging his individuality in answering the imperative of ritual purgation. The ritual purgation turns out to be a parody of the real thing.

Regaining consciousness after his fall, Kernan breaks away immediately from the circle of onlookers. Cunningham's scheme may have culminated in success, but Kernan up to the end still manages to preserve his own self-respect by refusing to use candles. Whether some genuine change has really occurred in Kernan's self, as evidenced by his grudging consent to participate in the retreat, can be verified in the last scene. Kernan and his friends are united with the generally condemned Harford, a fact that annihilates any shade of difference between the virtuous helpers and the ungrateful Harford. It seems that the light of "grace," here suggested by the "distant speck of red light" suspended before the high altar, fails to illumine Kernan.

The spectacle in the church proves instructive in determining the ultimate direction of our feelings toward the protagonist. For now we perceive indications that the retreat and its participants betray a divinely sanctioned hypocrisy that plagues Dublin's inhabitants. The retreat turns out to be a social function, a mere show, reinforcing the tribal habit of doing things together for material prosperity. Restoration of innocence, or renewal of faith, here means rededication to an ethic of worldly success—what Kernan as impoverished merchant urgently needs. Shown to be undisturbed by any feeling of trumpery, oblivious of the odd presence of Harford, Kernan arouses in us a punitive desire which the retreat does not assuage. Indifference and unquestioning trust in the group make Kernan one of those believers who, though implicitly pledged to a vision of an ideal world of transcendent perfection, nonetheless submit to the conventions of a secular society.

The narrative, as pointed out earlier, shifts from Kernan to Father Purdon and his sermon. This change of focus prevents us from directing our punitive desire against the absurdities of Kernan and his friends, and deflects emotion by presenting instead a difficult intellectual problem. Instead of an action or character, we are confronted with an intellectual topic: hermeneutics, the methods of interpretation of Scripture. The preacher appeals to the worldly-wise and calls for rectification of errors. But in excising his ambiguous text, an act similar to the misquotations of Kernan's friends, he provides a rationalization for secular compromise with Mammon. His tone of resonant assurance helps to coax the hearers to get rid of their qualms about "living in and for" the world. His rhetoric makes it appear that Christ's divine understanding supports his counsel in "setting before them as exemplars in the religious life those very worshippers of Mammon who were of all men the least solicitous in matters religious." That is, of course, a mistake. For if we compare the complete text of the parable with the lines quoted by the priest, we shall discover that the Mammon-worshippers are negative "exemplars," so that what Father Purdon asks from the community of the faithful is exactly the opposite of the imperious demand for categorical commitment, a choice of Mammon or Christ, addressed by Jesus to his disciples in Luke 16:8–13:

8   And the lord commended the unjust steward, because he

had done wisely: for the children of this world are in their
generation wiser than the children of light.

9 And I say unto you, Make to yourselves friends of the
mammon of unrighteousness; that, when ye fail, they may
receive you into everlasting habitations.

10 He that is faithful in that which is least is faithful also
in much: and he that is unjust in the least is unjust also
in much.

11 If therefore ye have not been faithful in the unrighteous
mammon, who will commit to your trust the true riches?

12 And if ye have not been faithful in that which is another man's, who shall give you that which is your own?

13 No servant can serve two masters: for either he will
hate the one, and love the other; or else he will hold to the
one, and despise the other. Ye cannot serve God and
mammon.

The preacher dissolves the mandate and its challenge by
a cunning dialectic, employing the analogy of business
accounts and converting the sinners into spiritual ac-
countants. He assumes that this will be the most suitable
language to communicate with pawnbrokers, usurers, poli-
ticians; but his conception of the Lord's ministry as
exemplified in the Parable of the Unjust Steward destroys
the sense of crisis and immediacy in the text, sanctioning
in turn a bourgeois complacency mimicked by his bar-
gaining style, his simplifications, his homely prudence.

   How easy it seems to deserve grace and salvation! Father
Purdon's little drama of the accountant who fixed his
debts to tally with his credits—a parodic version of the
sacrament—parallels the equivocation of Kernan's friends.
The priest's casuistic apology helps justify the businessmen's acceptance of the devil and his works. (Power's
early remark that "all's well that ends well"—a pun on
the Shakespearean-looking face of Cunningham—suggests
an unintended spoofing of the whole business.) This
technique of completing the action of the story with the

priest's sermon produces a caustic effect in which we somehow feel that justice has not been rendered to the guilty
party.

Joyce's singular aptitude for the selection of sensuous
details works to sharpen his dramatized scenes. His
methods of analogy and oblique reference prove efficient
instruments of representation when they are construed
as part of the dramatic economy of the action, which
demands a minimum of comment and the maximum of
signs from which we can draw inferences. The narrator's
heavy reliance on the reader's ability to draw inferences
intensifies the shock of recognition that we experience
when we formulate our assessment of the moral worth of
the protagonist and other agents in the story. Any statement with symbolic content in the narrative acquires
formal value if the multiple connections it can establish
aid in universalizing the scope of the situations, make
probable the sequence of events, or add to the appropriateness of thought, character, or incidents as means to
realize the purpose of the narrative. But what makes
possible our critical perception of values and norms is
the action itself, with its moral and emotional specifications.

Part V
Catharsis

15
THE DEAD

IT IS GENERALLY AXIOMATIC BY NOW TO CONCEIVE OF
critical understanding as an intellectual activity determined by various contexts and coordinates, the most
important of which is the end or purpose for which criticism is a means. On a *surview*—to borrow Coleridge's
suggestive term—of the field, the objects of our attention
fall into an intelligible pattern. Indeed, *surview* already
implies the presence of an organizing force behind objects
and processes vaguely sensed at first but gradually coher-
ing later. It involves thus the apprehension of *Gestalten*.
In his essay "On Method," Coleridge explains the intuitive cognition of a formal cause in the process of
composition: "It is the unpremeditated and evidently
habitual arrangement of [Shakespeare's] words, grounded
on the habit of foreseeing, in each integral part, or (more
plainly) in every sentence, the whole that he then intends
to communicate." Kant's whole metaphysical endeavor
was primarily addressed to elucidating the process of
cognition, a project which solves Hume's predicament
of being unable to render consistent two principles,
namely: ". . . that all our distinct perceptions are distinct
existences, and that the mind never perceives any real

connection among distinct existences" (*Treatise of Human Nature*).

Pursuing the idealistic response of German metaphysics to the empiricist's problem of relation among sense-data, Croce reconciles the traditional duality of form and matter by a "logical *a priori* concept" of art, and thus annihilates all need to distinguish literary works as organic wholes by subsuming them within a blanket principle: "Works of art exist only in the minds that create or recreate them." It is easy to see that Croce would be unable to point out exactly where the virtue of a particular literary form inheres, simply because he does not care to make the prior fundamental distinction between objects of nature and the artifices produced by men. It is likewise clear that since (to paraphrase Coleridge) phenomena can never yield a principle of definition and an explanation of part-whole relationships, we must seek for a speculative instrument that will not explain away the problem but grasp it in its complex objectivity. An accurate statement of the problem with reference to the conflicting explications of "The Dead" will be a first step toward the illustration of a method and the implicit principles necessary for this particular task.

The task here is simply put: What kind of "whole" is "The Dead"? The question implies a need to identify the elements or parts that constitute the whole, in what manner they are combined and for what ends, and, more decisively, the experience of the form itself as a result of the interaction between parts and whole—the life of harmony among parts in the whole form. We are here directly engaged in Hume's problem of "distinct existences" and their "connections." The crucial factor in the problem, the key element, appears to be the role of consciousness in the perception of "distinct existences" and their significant contexts.

Such philosophical issues will concretely reveal themselves as ultimate terms of difference and incompatibility. But differences obtain only if there is a common ground of understanding, when two positions participate in a common frame of reference. Where two positions conform to entirely contradictory sets of assumption, the clarification will lead to distinguishing *Weltanschauungen* or systems of viewing the world. On the other hand, if two positions claim to be engaged in achieving the same end, though by different procedures or techniques of schematizing, the clarification of differences will show us where validity of interpretation lies. How valid are the existing interpretations of "The Dead" as answers to the question of what kind of formal pattern or artifice "The Dead" exemplifies? Before venturing my interpretation, I would like to comment briefly on the major approaches critics have taken in analyzing the story.

In his essay "Three Definitions," Kenneth Burke outlines the stages in "The Dead" by focusing on the quantitative parts, each part performing the function of demonstrating his hypothesis: "the transcending of conditions, the ideal abandoning of property."[1] The stages in the story dramatize the movement from the realm of realism to the realm of ideality. But these stages do not follow the plot; they do not coincide with the structure of incidents except to block chronological sequence. The very word *plot* implies the sequence of cause-effect and the establishment of grounds of probability. Burke ignores the functions of beginning, middle, and end.

Burke's interest lies in proving his theory that the organizing principle of "The Dead" depends on the ending. Thus, if one accurately analyzes the import of the last paragraphs, one can define *a posteriori* the structure of the story. In essence, his analysis involves a form of inference by reduction: the justification of premises on the basis of

1. See Kenneth Burke's "Three Definitions," *Perspectives by Incongruity* (Bloomington, Ind.: Indiana University Press, 1964), pp. 142–51.

conclusions drawn from them. His theory hinges on a
translation into abstract terms of certain implications
drawn from the conclusion. Like other commentators,
Burke seizes on the predominant image of the snow and
its symbolic nuances to reinforce his "dramatistic" perspective. Burke argues first that Gabriel's "action," the
whole motivation of his existence, consists in his constant
progression from finite commitment (social attitudes, humors, etc.) to a transcending of the world of conditions
and ultimate arrival at the realm of the unconditioned:

> once we have been brought to this stage of "generosity,"
> where Gabriel can at last arrive at the order of ideal sociality,
> seeing all living things in terms of it, we return to the topic
> of snow, which becomes the mythic image, in the world of
> conditions, standing for the transcendence above the con-
> ditioned . . . "Upon the living and the dead." That is, upon
> the two as merged. That is, upon the world of conditions as
> seen through the spirit of conditions transcended, of ideal
> sociality beyond material divisiveness.[2]

What Burke has clearly ignored, to the great demerit of
his cogent analysis, is, first, the contextual charge of diction and imagery in the work, and, second, the subsidiary
functions of parts as diction and imagery in relation to
thought—the subordination of thought to character and
of character to plot. Foregoing the hierarchy of parts,
Burke isolates the image of "snow" and expands its import into a "mythic" element. While he observes that the
snow is an impression evolving into a generalized phenomenon within a particular setting, he forgets the nature
of the consciousness apprehending the image. "Ideal so-
ciality" can hardly be attributed to a man about to fall
asleep, and scarcely can one deduce Gabriel's equalization
of everything in his experience by mediation of a finite

---

2. *Ibid.*, pp. 150–51.

thing, the snow. For what actually happens is a transposition of intentional object: Gabriel's consciousness points
to nature unlocalized, to the dimension of existence as
physical (death equals the absence of life), in any case, to
a consciousness of time and space as the conditions determining consciousness itself.

Apart from the presence of other modes of transcending
the finite world—the ritual of celebration, music, Gretta's
silhouette apperceived by Gabriel's aesthetic intuition as
"Distant Music," the stylized dances, and the like—the
other questionable inference is the meaning for which
"the living and the dead" is supposed to stand. Echoing
Burke, Richard Ellmann in his biography of Joyce suggests that the snow represents "mutuality, a sense of the
connection with one another of the living and the dead, a
sense that none has his being alone."[3] The connective
"and" may be construed to support the unity between
these two opposing states which are receivers of the action
of falling snow. But viewed from the middle of the story
(which has resolved most of the possibilities in the beginning and which now generates momentum for resolution
at the end), who are "the living" and who are "the dead"?
Some critics have described Gabriel as the living dead,
while the dead—tradition, Michael Furey, the past in general—prove alive as efficient causes of the doing, thinking,
and feeling of the characters in the party. Depending on
the shift of qualifying contexts, "living" and "dead" spell
out levels of significations beyond the immediate syntax of
the paragraph. Even disregarding the loose and precarious
definitions of those equivocal elements, we note that
Burke and others have not given us any indication of
exactly where the *telos* of the parts and their interaction
lies, or what form of experience finds analogic representation in "The Dead."

---

3. *James Joyce* (New York: Oxford University Press, 1959), p. 260.

Preoccupation with dialectic movements in fiction leads to consigning formal elements to categories of ideas or thematic universals, so that in effect the work loses meaning as a unique configuration of experience which is nonetheless divisible into intelligible parts. Burke's procedure illustrates what his strategy can and cannot do. In comparison, the New Critical approach proves even more limiting. While it is certainly commendable of critics like Ransom and Brooks to insist on applying the principle of textual analysis, concentrating on the formal pattern as the main concern of aesthetic evaluation, the problem arises of determining the kind of formal pattern one is after and the conception of the work as a whole. The formalist's elevation of diction and image to first importance in the scale of parts has followed from Croce's equation of intuition and expression, and from a misunderstanding of Coleridge's notion of "Idea" as a "concrete universal" yet with identifiable parts. Ransom's and Wimsatt's notions of the "concrete universal" fail to account for the peculiar nature of a literary work as a composition of formally distinct parts. Consider now the remarks of Caroline Gordon and Allen Tate (in *The House of Fiction*) on the controlling metaphor of "The Dead," the clue to the organic integration of the whole:

> The overall symbol, the snow, which we first see as a scenic detail on the toe of Gabriel's galoshes, gradually expands until at the end it gathers up the entire action. The snow is the story. It is not necessary to separate its development from the dramatic structure or to point out in detail how at every moment, including the splendid climax, it reaches us through the eye as a naturalistic feature of the background. Its symbolic operation is of greater importance.[4]

The commentators here seem obsessed with the snow as a

---

4. *The House of Fiction* (New York: Scribners, 1950), pp. 281-82.

symbolic agency capable of conveying the essence of form,
or serving as the vehicle for the harmony of all parts of
the work. Clearly the mistake lies in overdetermining the
significance of a detail, and reducing the form of the story
to a drastic formula. What we really get in loading a detail
of the setting with a tremendous amount of associations
is an imposed allegorical signification—which does not
answer our fundamental question of part and whole.

One can multiply examples of the mistake the formalist
habitually commits, stemming from the denial of proportion by exaggerating the role of a part and making part
and whole somehow equivalent. An instance of compound-
ing the error is that of inflating an item, e.g., "galoshes,"
or even the clusters of bird-imagery and flower-imagery,
in order to reach by induction a vision of the working
of the parts. Carried to extremes, we get an observation
like Hugh Kenner's: "The fragrant air Gabriel had carried
into the Misses Morkan's house is the principle of death;
it is his proper medium, as he comes to see." Exercising
his acumen in a catalogue of random comments, the
explicator may be liable to fall straight into Hume's
dilemma or degenerate into inane virtuosity. One last
type of critical approach may be called quasi-philosophical,
taking "The Dead" as a result of applying the concept of
"epiphany" to experience. One can label this the "pedantic
fallacy," a trait readily observed in numerous studies. To
supplement and correct the imbalance of previous interpretations of "The Dead," I attempt here a new reading
in the hope of ascertaining the formal principle of the
story conceived as an "imitation of action," a significant
whole composed of meaningful parts.

The structure of the action imitated by "The Dead"
is complex, including a discovery and a reversal, with
Gabriel's acquisition of knowledge precipitating a change
of fortune through a process of purgation of consciousness. The action is chiefly the result of the convergence of

two movements: first, the sequence of incidents where
Gabriel figures as the chief actor; and second, the sequence
of adjustments in the situation, conveyed by imagery and
allusions, which present Gabriel's character, his power
of choice, his thoughts and feelings and utterances. Imagery and other iconographical details subserve the end of
embodying character in action. Toward the ending, after
the party (where Gabriel's hesitations are triumphantly
resolved in the dinner speech) and in the hotel room
(where his hesitations acutely worsen his plight) when
Gretta reveals the cause of her distraction, these two sequences combine and interact, exhausting all possibilities
of action and response in the protagonist. Gabriel's consciousness, at first directed on an object of passion, now
expands and breaks out from the impasse of oppressive
sentiment. A lyrical coda, comprising the pathos of the
action, is rendered with close-up and panoramic "shots"
that unify the inner self and the external world.

Everything then (all the incidents, the interplay among
characters making up the incidents, the thoughts as expressed in appropriate diction) will be seen to contribute
functionally toward Gabriel's sudden ecstatic affection for
his wife—the proof of his pride, inner darkness, and his
limited comprehension. The reversal proper consists of the
recognition of excess, the knowledge of a lack of objective
justification for his previous opinions, and the commensurate retribution dealt him. The reversal stems from his
awareness of his wife's genuine disposition toward him,
her past, and what this flawed attachment implies in regard to his social and historical existence. Knowledge
gained enables Gabriel to understand the necessary sequence of preceding events in his life at that particular
moment dealt with in "The Dead."

Portrayed from the inside, Gabriel defines the general
situation of the story, the issues and values rendered in
the thoughts and actions of the various personages, as well

as the range of attitudes and feelings that motivate their words and actions. Portrayed from the outside, the other characters—the two Aunts, Freddy Malins, and others—provide obstacles and reasons for frustration, of opportunities and their fulfillment, for incipient tendencies in the plot. One will observe that Gabriel's presence involves an action larger than the one he controls—indeed, his stature is shown as severely limited: most of the actions surrounding him escape his attention or his possible influence. Often he selects just a few objects and persons to act upon. In short, the action primarily progresses to define Gabriel's limitations and possibilities. Now, since the plot develops mainly to achieve a definite effect—certain emotions evoked by our inferences drawn from perceiving the actions constituting the plot—it is requisite to venture first a conception of the story's form in terms of an intention that animates the whole.

The composition of the story follows loosely the pattern of a formal elegy by its adherence to certain technical devices usually belonging to the literary convention of this genre, construed in a very general sense. It is profitable (although not relevant to my exposition of the "action") to delineate in the episodes the elements corresponding to the lament (the panegyric for the past, nostalgic reminiscences) —a festival-celebration of renewal (flowers, food, song), numerous descriptions alluding to "the dead" (candles, embroidery, statues), and the ubiquitous meditation on origins and destiny (Gabriel's inner monologue throughout). The social gathering at the Morkans on New Year's eve, with the ironically named "Three Graces" presiding and Gabriel declining to play the judge, turns out to be an occasion for retrospect and prophecy, for a judgment on the past, the present, and the future. All these are condensed in Gabriel's speech, elegantly designed and seriously meant—a rhetorical turning-point, a comic microcosm of reversal contained within the larger

tragic peripety of the whole work. The speech marks the
point where we can locate a counterpart to the movement
that begins shortly before Gabriel beholds his wife on
the stair. The speech is the end of the beginning, the
middle part of the story, with Gabriel's reason for being
present in the party being thus fulfilled.

We may also consider the speech as part of the elegiac
mode of extolling the virtues of the dead past, suggesting
the need for a forward-looking dedication to the present
and the future in order to perpetuate or immortalize the
glory of the past. Moreover, the speech neatly outlines all
the complications preceding its utterance. It witnesses to
the need for a sacramental propitiation of all those forces
that resist reason and will. Exhorting the listeners to
persevere in present duties and accept prospective challenge, Gabriel at the same time directs all thoughts to
the life of the immediate present. In relation to Gabriel's
sensibility at the end and its expanding horizon, the
speech, liberally generous and sympathetic to all, lays
down the probability for Gabriel's emotional fortune at
the end.

It is, of course, the life of the immediate circumstance
that the narrator dramatizes from the start by establishing
his distance from the fortune of the protagonist. The
narrator never identifies with the protagonist except in
passion-filled moments; the ironical-realistic tone requires
constant maintenance of distance. Lily, apart from being
an efficient housemaid, functions in this context as the
first antagonist to Gabriel's expectations. Lily's name suggests the floral emblem of the Archangel Gabriel who, in
Christian tradition, announced the coming of Christ to
Mary and who will announce the second coming of Christ.
The flower, signifying the coalescence of death and rebirth, is an inference derived from the dramatic situation
of the story. I hasten to warn the reader that all these
associations, now common knowledge, operate on the

second level of plot as a sequence of technical devices—
part of diction and thought—not fully in accord with the
straight progression of the action. In fact they often support a countermovement to the main action involving
Gabriel's self-exposure and catharsis.

Lily functions as usher, literally in the story and formally in the narrative frame. Major participants, setting,
and atmosphere are thus aptly conveyed by means of the
frame. A caretaker's daughter, she is conscientiously obe-
dient to Gabriel's fussy aunts. Concern for Gabriel's de-
layed arrival terminates at the fourth paragraph; Lily's
alert greeting leads to his notice of her complexion, her
hair, and a recall of their previous contact: "Gabriel had
known her when she was a child and used to sit on the
lowest step nursing a rag doll." This fact introduces the
motif of change (of posture, position, states, conditions)
as topic of thought. The principal movement of reversal
is epitomized in Lily's ambiguous role, in the thought
about her (see Aunt Kate's opinion), in the spectacle
(bathrooms converted to dressing-room), and in the diction. *Palaver,* from late Latin meaning "parable," used
to denote a long parley usually between persons of different levels of culture and sophistication, a real dialogue,
has degenerated to other usages: idle chatter, misleading
speech, cajolery, and the like. Examples of other transposi-
tions in word-sense (changes from outside to inside, and
vice versa) may easily be accumulated.

Intimacy, prompted by the previous acquaintance of
Gabriel and Lily, is to be disrupted by a description of
the man's appearance. The pattern and rhythm of this
single scenic part epitomizes the entire development of the
plot insofar as Gabriel is the effective agent:

—Tell me, Lily, he said in a friendly tone, do you still go
to school?
—O no, sir, she answered. I'm done schooling this year and
more.

—O, then, said Gabriel gaily, I suppose we'll be going to
your wedding one of these fine days with your young man, eh?
The girl glanced back at him over her shoulder and said
with great bitterness:

—The men that is now is only all palaver and what they can
get out of you.

Gabriel coloured, as if he felt he had made a mistake and,
without looking at her, kicked off his galoshes and flicked
actively with his muffler at his patent-leather shoes.

Contrast the young men nowadays and Michael Furey,
the sacrificed lover of Gretta in her reminiscence. After
that bit of conversation, a description of Gabriel's appearance and his effort to induce self-assurance by a
patronizing act follows:

> When he has flicked lustre into his shoes he stood up and
> pulled his waistcoat down more tightly on his plump body.
> Then he took a coin rapidly from his pocket.
> —O Lily, he said, thrusting it into her hands, it's Christmas-
> time, isn't it? Just . . . here's a little. . . .
> He walked rapidly towards the door.
> —O no, sir! cried the girl, following him. Really, sir, I
> wouldn't take it.
> —Christmastime! Christmastime! said Gabriel, almost trot-
> ting to the stairs and waving his hand to her in deprecation.
> The girl, seeing that he had gained the stairs, called out
> after him:
> —Well thank you, sir.

In the above passages we find in minutiae an expectation ventured and balked, a temporary break and a forced
resolution. The episode serves as the symmetrical counterpart to the Gabriel-Gretta "catechism" at the end and its
rhythm of hope and disappointment. Gabriel's feeling ("as
if he had made a mistake") thus qualified points to his
physical presence as a cause of movement in dialogue. He
accidentally reveals Lily's true personality, her bitter feel-

ing and dissatisfaction concealed beneath the façade of routine she tries to preserve. Aunt Kate verifies Lily's changed manner in her remark: "She's not the girl she was at all"—the motif of change is clearly sounded there.

His confidence partly undermined, Gabriel forcibly contrives a reconciliation when he hands a coin which the girl refuses. Gabriel literally avoids the refusal by running up to the house, escaping with the feeble invocation of Christmas, his tone summed up in the phrase "in deprecation." Lily's role is defined in what she does to Gabriel, who upstairs finds himself "still discomposed by the girl's bitter and sudden retort. It had cast a gloom over him which he tried to dispel by arranging his cuffs and the bows of his tie." This attempt to recover composure by smoothing his dress to produce an impression of orthodox conformity succeeds, but only for a while.

Gabriel as central protagonist then thinks of his role as after-dinner speaker, inducing further motion of his will. Conflict between his desire to win admiration for his superior refinement and his desire to insure harmony for her Aunt's sake, or for decency's sake, emerges:

> The indelicate clacking of the men's heels and the shuffling of their soles reminded him that their grade of culture differed from his. He would only make himself ridiculous by quoting poetry to them which they could not understand. They would think that he was airing his superior education. He would fail with them just as he had failed with the girl in the pantry. He had taken up a wrong tone. His whole speech was a mistake from first to last, an utter failure.

Other matters interpose between the Lily-Gabriel and Gabriel-Miss Ivors misunderstandings: wizened Mr. Browne comes up. Enigmatically "brown," he puns on the prevalent color of the setting. By force of metonymy, he acts as the Dionysian "genius" of the place who supervises over wine, dance, food, and revelry. Viewed as a

personification of the absurd, he is scrupulously gre-
garious. Another spectacle is focused on Aunt Julia's
fright at Freddy Malin's entrance, signaling hostility to
the drunkard. In this context, Freddy is the Lord of Mis-
rule who enlivens the solstice consort of death and rebirth,
the saturnalia of myth celebrated in midwinter.

Gabriel's premonition of appearing a ridiculous and
pathetic victim of self-courted failure, insinuated by Lily's
rebuff, proves misleading: his tactfully calculated speech
evokes warm applause and leads to fervent praise of the
hostesses, however undercut the hyperboles are. All these
double-edged effects make prominent the ironic details
that deflate enthusiasm. Yet, on the whole, Gabriel's intention is energetically carried out. Toward a final conception of what he would say after dinner, one more
decisive encounter contributes: Gabriel's skirmish with
Miss Ivors, "a frank-mannered talkative young lady." She
engages Gabriel in a duel in which his naïveté and solemn
and restrained bearing give way to perplexity and anxious
defensiveness. Accused, he replies: "Why should I be
ashamed of myself?"

Since Miss Ivors has been a longtime friend and aca-
demic contemporary, Gabriel controls himself, unable to
adopt any fixed stance. Miss Ivors says that she's only
joking, but her needling advice about seeing the Aran
Isles and learning Gaelic provokes Gabriel's violent outburst that "Irish is not my language"—in multiple senses
of "language." He is finally led to the confession, "I'm
sick of my country, sick of it!" The impasse generated
here indicates the chief burden of Gabriel's mind, the
sustained conflict between what he thinks and presumes
he knows, and what reality is and what it has in store
for him. Undeterred by embarrassment, he plods on and
seeks the rationale of human conduct.

The clash between Miss Ivors and Gabriel unfolds the

image of a wrathful female spectre who calls attention to Gabriel's personality: all the women characters enact this role. Gretta, for example, finally defines for us Gabriel's capacity to comprehend, appraise, and gauge the manner and pressure of his actions. With Lily and Miss Ivors, however, he withdraws from direct confrontation (unlike his persistent questioning of Gretta), wishing to establish rapport and preserve peace during the party. Nonetheless, the action of other personages forces him to decide by earnest response or noncommital evasion:

> Gabriel tried to cover his agitation by taking part in the dance with great energy. He avoided her eyes for he had seen a sour expression on her face.

Miss Ivors manifests an ambiguous position: she charges and withdraws. She behaves erratically, like a taunting jester: "But when they met in the long chain he was surprised to feel his hand firmly pressed. She looked at him from under her brows for a moment quizzically until he smiled." But following the ritual movement of the dance, she whispers: "West Briton!"

The dance over, Gabriel turns to Freddy Malin's mother. His mind once more obsessively revolves around the anticipated blunder he might commit, the fear that he might cut a ridiculous figure:

> Of course the girl or woman, or whatever she was, was an enthusiast but there was a time for all things. Perhaps he ought not to have answered her like that. But she had no right to call him a West Briton before people, even in joke. She had tried to make him ridiculous before people, heckling him and staring at him with her rabbit's eyes.

The accompanying stylized motion of the personages in the dance dramatizes the fluctuation of tension mirrored in the tone of the utterances, and in the thoughts, feelings, and appetitive advance and retreat of the whole moral being of the characters.

All the time, one senses a continuing modification in the relation between Gabriel and Gretta. Talking to his aunts about Gabriel's precautions for her health and his commands, Gretta says: "He's really an awful bother. . . ." Then, with Miss Ivor's baiting, his attitude toward visiting Galway becomes fixed. And his negative stance to Miss Ivors contaminates his reply to his wife:

> —You can go if you like, said Gabriel coldly.
> She looked at him for a moment, then turned to Mrs. Malins and said:
> —There's a nice husband for you, Mrs. Malins.

Pointed irony, addressed to Mrs. Malins, thwarts the husband's expectation. For Gabriel's regard, frozen into a fixed dislike for Miss Ivors, can no longer discriminate between bigoted Nationalist and wife. The surprise he mutely registers displays the typical working of his presence on the situation and on the people around him. Once this is clearly understood, the dynamic schema underlying the system of actions in the whole plot reveals itself.

A moment before his carving the goose, Gabriel assumes a willed distance from society by projecting his consciousness to the external world. He feels oppressed by the demands of his environment. Faced by a circumstance with unknown threats in the offing, Gabriel feels severely estranged. In contrast, the wintry world outside, an alienating and hostile force at the beginning, now offers a spacious and comfortable haven for Gabriel's spirit. He is reconciled with nature's elements; he moves toward a middle position with his newly attained poise: "How pleasant it would be to walk out alone. . . . How much more pleasant it would be there than at the supper table's." The pictorial rendition connects with the closing idyllic panorama of snow "general over Ireland" in scope and affective resonance. Wellington Monument, enduring memorial to infamy, loses its negative quality, not because of the snow covering it, but because of the changing sensibility of the character. Unless it reflects the flux of feelings and attitudes, the landscape has no significance for the developing action of the story. Landscape intentionally conceived betrays its significance only in relation to characters with whom it is related by metaphoric parallelism (analogy) or metonymic participation (contiguity). Granted this mode of reading, all other details—galoshes, picture on the wall, goose, coffin-like cab, candle, grated window, crosses in the cemetery, and so on—are refracted by the sensibility of the characters they are acting upon, or by characters acting upon them.

Gabriel then returns to his speech and frames a sarcastic allusion to Miss Ivors, an act of courageous defiance. But with her departure, Gabriel cancels his challenge and subdues his belligerent tone. He tries to affirm his friendship by volunteering to see her home, but she refuses. Doubtful of himself as cause of her leaving, Gabriel "stared blankly down the staircase"—an attitude repeated by his wife, but with a more serious consequence. Participation with the group ensues. Gabriel recedes into the background while conversation turns alternately on Aunt Julia and Aunt Kate, the music of the past, Aunt Julia's expulsion from the choir, and the like. This momentary absence of Gabriel is needed so as to facilitate the countermovement to his joyful and fiery affection for his wife on their way home; such a countermovement, made up of divisive tastes, the praise of the past as more splendid than the present, and the motif of religious asceticism, thus accumulates a potent charge in its impact with Gabriel's desire for union. Obviously Gabriel's momentary withdrawal is part of a modulation of his climactic presiding over the festive scene.

The highlight of the party centers on Gabriel, as the chosen protagonist, officiating in carving the main dish and acting as spokesman of the guests. The collective rejoicing harmonizes the distorting agents—for example, Freddy Malins and Mr. Browne—though, before final departure, Bartell D'Arcy will again sound the note of discord to presage the cross-purposes and discrepancy of moods that spoil the husband-and-wife intimacy. At this point, however, the essence of unity crystallizes in Gabriel's speech. Before he performs this ritual of exorcising the ghostly past vividly evoked in the conversation among the guests—for he wants to deliver the present from the bondage of the past while extolling the "Furies"—he makes the appeal "kindly forget my existence." Then he lets the party evolve by its own momentum. Talk about music and monks blends innocence and bliss with ascetic denial, sacrifice, and suffering. The pause naturally heightens our anticipation of what Gabriel is actually going to say. His oration resolves all the tensions engendered by the preceding conflicts. It shows how in fact Gabriel's series of disappointments (with Lily, Miss Ivors, his aunts, and his wife) is required for this end. If logically flawed, the speech is perfectly consistent with our idea of Gabriel's character: easily disturbed, yet capable of imposing discipline on himself; sensitive; willful; intelligent. The speech compresses all these traits into a rhetorical composite, with all the subtle devices of qualification tactfully operating.

In executing his function to everybody's delight and the aunts' pleasure, Gabriel seeks a reflection of his identity as successful and responsible citizen. Order, self-confidence, and decorum characterize his speech; his estimate of past, present, and future impresses all as fair and just. He provides a basis for a smooth, convivial departure of the guests in spite of Freddy Malin's burlesque gestures with the fork (suggesting his aspect as King of the Dead and the Underworld). The ironic mode of presentation mixes levels of style, the serious and the parodic, the mean and the lofty. The action of recognition after the reversal of Gabriel's fortune prescribes the ironic treatment of the serious events in the party.

Having regained his balance and effected a temporary accord among the celebrants, Gabriel can afford to joke. Pantomime and caricature release anxiety, guilt, anger, pity, and the sense of humiliation. Gabriel's humor restores everybody's feeling of security, with the past itself affording material for detached citation. Gabriel has partly dissolved his fear of being ridiculous by projecting it to a past incident, using death (represented by Patrick Morkan and his servile horse) to purge his inner hindrances, the psychic block that prevents the intensification of his attachment with others. But before leaving, Gabriel senses a new threat, suggested by his wife's posture, the song recording grief over a child's death, the at-first-unidentified musicians. Just as in an early scene he had looked up at the pantry ceiling to note the disturbance upstairs and "listened for a moment to the piano," so now Gabriel repeats the pose, but with a telling difference. Unable to share in his wife's listening, he strains to apprehend the unknown—that hardly audible music—which has transformed his wife, no longer a bodily presence but an incandescent figure combining time (music) and space (distance)—a synesthetic whole afforded by Gabriel's intuition. Note the changed disposition of Gabriel as the sight of his wife yields a vision of a transcendent presence. I submit that the "epiphanic" moment occurs precisely here, the later self-disillusionment being an elaborate continuation:

He was in a dark part of the hall gazing up the staircase. A woman was standing near the top of the first flight, in the shadow also. He could not see her face but he could see the terra-cotta and salmon-pink panels of her skirt which the shadow made appear black and white. It was his wife. She was leaning on the banisters, listening to something. Gabriel was surprised at her stillness and strained his ear to listen also. But he could hear little save the noise of laughter and dispute on the front steps, a few chords struck on the piano and a few notes of a man's voice singing.

He stood still in the gloom of the hall, trying to catch the air that the voice was singing and gazing up at his wife. There was grace and mystery in her attitude as if she were a symbol of something. He asked himself what is a woman standing on the stairs in the shadow, listening to distant music, a symbol of. If he were a painter he would paint her in that attitude. Her blue felt hat would show off the bronze of her hair against the darkness and the dark panels of her skirt would show off the light ones. *Distant Music* he would call the picture if he were a painter.

Observe the suspended or still-life quality of Gretta's image, the lapidary shading of color that makes her sculpturesque radiance in Gabriel's eyes somehow apocalyptic. Indeed, the song rescurrects the memory of the dead Michael in Gretta's mind.

Gabriel's detachment is momentary. Bartell D'Arcy's rude conduct destroys the precarious equilibrium won by his jesting and intrudes the notion of winter and snow as a hostile force by the mention of his affliction. But Gabriel's attention is still fixed on his wife. He is plunged into quiet brooding; then, when Gretta turns to him, "Gabriel saw that there was colour on her cheeks and that her eyes were shining. A sudden tide of joy went leaping out of his heart." This rapturous awareness, made surprising but probable by his clowning acts and his detached observations, induces a recall of the past and lifts Gabriel's

consciousness far from the ugly distortions of the present
moment. This lyrical mood becomes the vehicle for affirming life and for the sustaining power of love, which
resists the encroachment of custom and outmoded usage.
The past overflows into the present, radically converting
Gabriel's attitude into benign, selfless generosity. He
proves himself superior to the absolute force of opinion
by this realization of an emotional possibility. And his
character, moving toward a confrontation with his wife,
is to demonstrate its inexhaustible resources as it experiences a recognition of its limitations and of the larger
purpose underlying experience. The movement pursues
a straight course, manifesting Gabriel's range of suscepti-
bilities until it is halted by the lack of appropriate response: "She had no longer any grace of attitude, but
Gabriel's eyes were still bright with happiness. The blood
went bounding along his veins; and the thoughts went
rioting through his brain, proud, joyful, tender, valorous."
Gretta, in Gabriel's vision, possesses the awe of "grace
and mystery," attributes which attest to his ability to
project Gretta and Michael in a dramatic setting later,
identifying himself with his antagonist and thus resolving
conflict.

At this juncture, recollection of their honeymoon occasions Gabriel's thoughts of journey, quest, and the ordeal
of passage. The crescendo of his emotion proceeds to the
point when it is broken by the porter's ominous shadow,
the ghastly (originally "ghostly") light from the street
lamp, and Gretta's weary face. A subtle modulation from
courteous to casual exchange, and then to Gretta's mention of Gabriel's generosity, prepares the revelation of
Gabriel's insufficiency, the unreason of his job, and his
proud intellect. Self-estrangement follows: "As he passed
in the way of the cheval-glass he caught sight of himself
in full length, his broad well-filled shirt-front, the face
whose expression always puzzled him when he saw it in a

mirror, and his glimmering gilt-rimmed eyeglasses." That glimpse of himself objectified in the mirror resembles somewhat the description of his appearance after Lily's disconcerting retort. If Gabriel has any fault, it is un-witting ignorance. What will restore harmony between his consciousness and his behavior is a certain measure of detachment required for grasping a true knowledge of his own situation.

Irony doubles in a dialectic of question and answer between husband and wife, producing multiple reversals. Gabriel, craving closeness, uses tactics that recoil, widen-ing the distance between them. The fundamental irony, based on his ignorance of Gretta's early life, subtends the scene in the hotel room. Physical intimacy and Gabriel's desire emerge only after the impromptu exchange about Freddy Malin's recently repaid debt, which unexpectedly —since it was mentioned casually—inspires Gretta to praise Gabriel and kiss him. With admirable self-control, Gabriel pursues the inquisition of his true iden-tity. It is this unflinching courage investing his desire to know his real self that contributes the tragic quality to his character and forms the saving grace of his painful discovery of his utter insignificance:

> Gabriel felt humiliated by the failure of his irony and by the evocation of this figure from the dead, a boy in the gasworks. While he had been full of memories of their secret life to-gether, full of tenderness and joy and desire, she had been comparing him in her mind with another. A shameful con-sciousness of her own person assailed him. He saw himself as a ludicrous figure, acting as a pennyboy for his aunts, a nervous, well-meaning sentimentalist, orating to vulgarians and idealizing his clownish lusts, the pitiable fatuous fellow he had caught a glimpse of in the mirror. Instinctively he turned his back more to the light lest she might see the shame that burned upon his forehead.

The countermovement to the sequence, which includes
the snow as the deadly element, nationalist Ireland, the
dead past, tradition, the old songs, and Gabriel's superior
culture, now delivers its impact on the protagonist, who
is thereby rendered passive and devoid of will. Yet he remains conscious while the specter from the dead is summoned: "A vague terror seized Gabriel at this answer,
as if, at that hour when he had hoped to triumph, some
impalpable and vindictive being was coming against him,
gathering forces against him in its vague world. But he
shook himself free of it with an effort of reason and con-
tinued to caress her hand." In *A Portrait of the Artist as a
Young Man,* Stephen Dedalus defines terror as "the feeling which arrests the mind in the presence of whatsoever
is grave and constant in human sufferings and unites it
with the secret cause." Gabriel, with his artistic self
ascendant, experiences this aesthetic emotion of terror
and, by so doing, unites with Michael's phantom. The
hero's eclipse, caused by the avenging past resurrected in
Gretta's nostalgic melancholy, passes.

As a responsible agent, Gabriel effects a purgation of
his psyche by an act of sympathy. He is active throughout
until the moment he weeps, signaling the third stage of
the plot: pathos. Dramatic reversal of the hero's fortune
transforms his role from being mourner in vigil for all
the dead (when he delivers his speech) to one who enacts
his own processional. Gretta falls asleep, a metaphoric
passing away, which is comprehensible on the literal
plane. Gabriel's attitude, supported by a lucid awareness
of the causes of his wife's dejection, becomes "unresent-
ful." Freed from self-ignorance and the unwarranted assumption of vanity, he assumes the viewpoint of observer
of his wife's private life. Preserving distance, Gabriel
exercises aesthetic discrimination of the feelings and
values involved in his wife's past. His wife's past life

excludes him completely. No longer a participant and
no longer anxious about attacks against his ego and the
peril of self-mockery, he can depend on his own detachment, which spontaneously begets a poised and sensitive
registration of actuality:

> It hardly pained him now to think how poor a part he, her
> husband, had played in her life. He watched her while she
> slept, as though he and she had never lived together as man
> and wife. His curious eyes rested long upon her face and on
> her hair: and, as he thought of what she must have been,
> then, in that time of her first girlish beauty, a strange,
> friendly pity for her entered his soul.

He senses identity with the dead lover; he intuits a greater
force as his enemy—time, existence itself in time and
space, and ultimately the exigencies and contingencies of
human life. His insight into his wife's sentimental nature,
weighed against her aged face, vitalizes his process of re-
assessment: "He wondered at his riot of emotions. . . .
Poor Aunt Julia!" Like the rhythm of his speech, his
mind moves backward and forward in alternating retro-
spection and augury, converting the future into the past
and collapsing the barriers of time and space. His musings
about death intensify, bringing tears: "Generous tears
filled Gabriel's eyes. He had never felt like that himself
towards any woman, but he knew that such a feeling must
be love," and so forth, leading finally to the memorable
impressionistic luminosity at the end as soul and snow
swoon together. The spacious compass of the setting
serves as the proper theater for the dissolution of self and
the concrete expression of man's involvement in the unfolding of a larger cosmic or natural destiny.

The convergence of the two sequences of actions (the
secondary action can be designated as the subplot, if one
likes) —one, of incidents moved by, or which move, the

protagonist; the other, of thoughts, images, and symbolic analogues—transforms the character of Gabriel from one who is terribly engaged in constant adjustment between the world and his conception of himself and join one who is dominated by sentiment and yet avoids fixity, to one whose sympathy for his wife extends to her dead lover, to Aunt Julia—to the living and the dead—so that his consciousness, fusing with the snow enshrouding the whole world, annihilates all contradictions. Since consciousness undergoes a dialectic of resolving all conflicts, character loses substance if the tension caused by interacting sentiments and thoughts is not established right from the beginning (here, in Gabriel's distress over Lily's response). The development of events in a sequence culminates in a lyrical stasis, a pure melodic continuum, consonant with a disengagement of the self from the contradictions of finite existence. Indeed, all the causes of Gabriel's unrest, concentrated in the unsuspected treachery of a hidden past in his wife's life—a past whose recovery is accomplished by all the contributing forces in the action—are finally given articulate power in terms of their effects. Imagistic and rhetorical devices—like snow, the song, Mr. Browne, the goose served for dinner, and so on, which recur in dialogue and in the thoughts of the characters, and other elements that form part of the incidents deployed in time and space, occupying the horizontal and vertical dimensions of the story—reveal their integral functions in the light of the final sequence, the pathos or agony of Gabriel. The action of the story at this point, with all possibilities exhausted and everything organized in conformity with the sequence of the parts, appears complete.

CONCLUSION

TO DEFINE THE LIMITS OF THE ANALYSIS AND CRITICISM OF *Dubliners* would be to ascertain the infinitude of viewpoints and criteria the human intellect can contrive—a virtually impossible task. All theorizing on the powers of human nature for the purpose of prophesying its destiny seems gratuitous here in a study of the reasons why Joyce's stories have an enduring appeal, a staying vigor and newness. It might be more profitable and relevant, by way of summary to the interpretations offered in this book, to formulate certain general conclusions regarding the nature of Joyce's narrative craft, especially in terms of the species of art it produced and its distinctive effects. For the artist of *Dubliners* is distinguished above all by his gift of *making,* his capacity to make specific works that contain within themselves their own principles of integrity, in order to achieve very definite and specific ends.

It would be presumptuous to claim that the specific ends of a particular story, say "Eveline," can be fully articulated by Joyce's aim of presenting the paralysis syndrome, as I have argued in the introduction and in the chapters of this book. To enumerate again the commonplace themes of *Dubliners*—the Dantean vices, the symbolism of east and west, mythical analogies, even the

234

conjectured Homeric correspondences—would be super-
fluous. Most interpretations of *Dubliners* operate on the
premise that Joyce intended each story to be an exemplum, or an anecdote serving as a paradigm of a
thematic argument, and the characters as illustrative figures incarnating certain qualities or humors. Or else the
stories, say "Grace," are construed as a parody of the
Divine Comedy, equating pub with hell, home with purgatory, church with paradise. Instead of universalizing the
realistic details of the story, the allegorical fashion of
explicating the meaning of narrative action tends to reduce the range and depth of what one can say about the
reasons why Joyce's stories give a complex delight, a
pleasure that inheres in the way the story is put together.

Thus I have deliberately refrained from theorizing on
the whole pattern of *Dubliners* with either Dante or
Homer or Vico in mind. Unless we have first described
with accuracy what kind of a whole each story is—which,
after all, is what the artist produced to fulfill a specific
intention, for the artist never creates a general thing—all
speculation on the framework or subsuming archetype
of the whole book would be distractive and misleading.
In any case, it seems that a working hypothesis would have
to be invented to describe the book in its totality. Is it
essentially a collection of life-histories thematically related
to serve as the spiritual chronicle of a city? Or is it something else? Whether in subject or treatment, a new category or genre is needed to define the whole artwork called
Dubliners.

Joyce himself is not entirely blameless for encouraging
allegorical readings of his work. The introduction has
explored at length the value and relevance of the artist's
expressed intentions in relation to the final product he
has accomplished. What remains to be done now is to
classify the stories in terms of the *dominant* emotional
effects the plots bring about and, by the same token,

also classify the kinds of unifying action the stories possess.

As with all generalizing classifications, the primary or dominant attributes have priority. It is possible to classify all the stories as concerned with the "exposure of being," not the process of becoming, whereby the technique of exposing static situations becomes a vehicle for *anagnorisis*. Arnold Goldman, for example, contends that Joyce's focus on boundary or transitional situations leads to a thematic monism, resolving the opposition between fixity and dissociation by a mechanism of distortion, projection, condensation, displacement, and so on. After tracing the progressive alternation of themes, the oscillation of realism and romance, the rhythm of constraint and freedom in *Dubliners*, Goldman concludes that the linguistic situation or the style of the book is a function of the existential situation: "It is finally indifferent whether the environments are thematic reflections of characters' personalities (symbolic expressionism) or whether the personalities themselves are only functions of the environment (determinism)."[1] Consequently, the formulation of alternatives in the story is deliberately vague, if not ambiguous.

All fiction of any worth necessarily deals with existential situations, if by "existential" is meant a disclosure of how characters either recognize a truth about themselves in relation to their world, or recognize the essence of the human condition (as in "The Dead"), or suffer the world to reveal itself through their critical or developing consciousness (as in "The Sisters"). Fiction concerned with presenting a crisis in the protagonist's self, whether this crisis leads to a discovery and complete change or simply reiterates and underscores a typical and habitual mechanism in the personality, may be said to deal with existential situations. But it is doubtful whether such a descrip-

---

1. *The Joyce Paradox: Form and Freedom in His Fiction* (Evanston, Ill.: Northwestern University Press, 1966), p. 5.

tion can express anything about the specific effects aroused by a single story in *Dubliners*.

To assert that *Dubliners* exemplifies the phenomenology of existential crisis may explain one quality that aligns the book with the modernistic fashion of "zeroing in" on traumatic or spiritual dilemmas in narrative forms. But it scarcely defines the power of each story or the kind of artistic wholes Joyce created. Character as the power to act or choose, and setting as a device of representation, operate as means to organize our emotional responses in a way coordinate with the total movement of the plot. Environment and character acquire meaning only as functional elements of the story's unifying action.

A quick recall of the stories and the kind of changes rendered in the plots will give the impression that almost all the characters—except perhaps for the child-protagonist narrators in the first three stories—are inferior characters caught in ugly, compromising situations, their sufferings more or less caused by some distortion in their attitudes, which prove resistant to change. The sufferings of the characters prove needless but inescapable, since they are unable to correct the defects they come to recognize because of lack of will power, or because they are blind to their defects by virtue of their own nature.

In most cases, the pathetic or fearsome implications of the suffering or misfortune are distanced precisely by the general absence of notably admirable qualities in the character. This feature of Joyce's rhetorical strategy also weakens any potential or serious pity we might entertain toward the character. And since his deficiencies are not imminently harmful or destructive to any person other than himself, the protagonist does not arouse any serious fear or horror. On the whole, the development in the plot would then be from potential sympathy for the protagonist toward a decrease of sympathy; the final effect involves a judgment that he deserves the suffering he gets.

But the judgment on the protagonist's fate does not give a sense of relief, with an accompanying satisfaction of our punitive urge, because we generally feel that there is some underlying justice—either the prevalent corruption in the whole metropolis or the absence of any internal norm of goodness or sanity in the story—which dissolves all painful or pitiful effects.

This pattern of the caustic story as Austin McGiffert Wright first proposed and defined it may be confirmed by the analysis of "Grace" offered in this book, or by an inspection of the action of "A Little Cloud," "Ivy Day in the Committee Room," or "Two Gallants."[2] But this pattern needs modification. For unlike "Ivy Day," a caustic comedy with multiple protagonists, or "Grace," stories like "Clay," "A Mother," and "The Boarding House" present characters who are not without likable qualities when the moral nature of their problems is weighed against the alternatives of action offered them by their particular social situations. Joyce's delicate weighing of merits and defects sometimes precludes any definite condemnation or exoneration. Nor is it altogether accurate to state that all the stories fall under the category of "nonpainful" because the ultimate pleasure we get comes out of the avoidance of, or escape from, the threat of a painful experience. For stories like "A Mother" and, especially, "Counterparts" evoke a muted feeling of horror not wholly devoid of pain insofar as we side with the victim and his partially undeserved misfortune. In the conventional short story, the narrator's authority may be seen to manipulate the action in such a way that our identification of villain and hero of the stories will insure the exact distribution of sympathy and blame when the

2. I am indebted to Austin McGiffert Wright not only for the concept of the "caustic" short story but also for the general approach used in this book. See Wright's excellent work *The American Short Story in the Twenties* (Chicago: University of Chicago Press, 1961), especially pp. 205–16.

conflict is resolved in the end. No such thing can be found in any story in *Dubliners*.

To classify the stories in *Dubliners*, two criteria may be used. We can inquire first whether the story concerns an action, or an activity of character, of thought, or of feeling, and then we can proceed to determine the nature of the effect or emotional power which the story as a whole is intended to produce. The unifying action inheres in the plot or episodes being represented, the scale and proportion of representation, the sequence, and the like. It might be helpful to make the distinction that, whereas the plot unfolds a complete and irreversible change in the depicted situation, with the parts linked causally to bring about a change, an episode does not represent a completed action. The change involved in an episode is an incomplete change.

Each of the stories in *Dubliners* is essentially unified by a single episode. Technically, the term "episode" designates the action of situations centering about a principal event—to borrow Elder Olson's distinction—while the action of situations centering about more than one principal event may be designated the grand plot.[3] The episodes of a story are so designed as to stress different kinds of activity in order to modify the original fixed situation: for example, Eveline's choice (in "Eveline") removes one possibility of radically altering her life; Mrs. Mooney's decision (in "The Boarding House") spells a change in her family; the characters in "Ivy Day in the Committee Room" harden themselves despite the opportunity for acting differently at election time and during the celebration of Parnell's death anniversary. "Ivy Day" is centered on the exposure of a reiterated habitual choice and represents a change in the sense that a resurgent force of habit cripples or enfeebles the protagonists' will.

---

3. Elder Olson, *Tragedy and the Theory of Drama* (Detroit, Mich.: Wayne State University Press, 1966 reprint), p. 42.

In terms of the plot and the likelihood of the sequence of incidents, the stories in *Dubliners* show that no sequence is simply generated by the spectacle of incidents themselves without taking into account the probabilities of character. For if by plot we mean a system of actions of a determinate moral quality, then the artist must establish the moral worth of his agents to determine the affective meaning of the story. The meaning of the object imitated, and its affective significance as the force that gives form to its proper pleasure, derive from the moral quality disclosed and emphasized by the action.

In terms of the probability of the sequence of incidents and the origin of this probability, we can classify the plots of stories into three kinds: the plot of character, in which the likelihood of the sequence of incidents arises from the *ethos* of the protagonist, as in "Two Gallants," "The Boarding House," "Ivy Day in the Committee Room," "A Mother," and "Grace"; the plot of pathos, in which the intentions of the characters do not interfere with the progression of incidents and hence no reversal or recognition takes place, as in "Eveline," "After the Race," "A Little Cloud," "Counterparts," and "Clay"; and the stories with a complex activity, possessing stages of reversal and recognition, such as "The Sisters," "An Encounter," "Araby," "A Painful Case," and "The Dead."[4]

In the first three stories, dealing with childhood, self-discovery or self-revelation takes place (though the recognition is muted or displaced in "The Sisters" and can only be inferred from the protagonist's narration) in the protagonist as he undergoes an experience of crisis and initiation and comes to grips with reality. In a sense, even

4. For the types of plot used here, and other formal distinctions regarding the "imitation of action," see Kenneth Telford, *Aristotle's Poetics: Translation and Analysis* (Chicago: Regnery, 1961), pp. 59–143. Cf. Elder Olson's essay "The Poetic Method of Aristotle: Its Powers and Limitations," in *Aristotle's Poetics and English Literature* (Chicago: University of Chicago Press, 1965), pp. 175–91.

"A Painful Case" or "The Dead" may be said to initiate the adult into a higher level of maturity. But what chiefly distinguishes the first three stories from the rest is, of course, the capacity of the youthful protagonist to transcribe his surroundings faithfully and so reveal its limitations by his naïve or innocent perspective. Moreover, he is capable of detaching himself from the degenerate milieu by reason of his incomprehension, or he is capable of transcending it by his resilience and adaptability, his resourcefulness and honesty.

In "The Sisters," the disillusionment of the protagonist at the end generates pathos, for the boy awakens to the disparity between his thoughts and the actuality, without his conscious intentions exerting any influence on the direction of events. We have to infer that what he experiences will not be injurious to his well-being, but will instead exert a chastening influence on his future relations with people he enthusiastically admires. In "An Encounter," a sense of dread develops when the old simpleton begins to confess his love of whipping boys with sweethearts, but the terrifying potentiality there is subdued when the narrative focuses on the boy's penitent attitude, hinting just enough to allay our fear that the old man will hurt him. Both pathos and dread characterize the effect of "Araby," though a calm and intellectualized conclusion that indicates the boy's capacity for detachment modulates the fearful implications of his disappointment by attributing the cause of the frustration to the protagonist's failure to temper his grandiose expectations and moderate his romantic feelings.

The next four stories, centering on adolescence, heighten the effect of pathos by showing how the intentions of the characters are either depreciated or ignored by the inimical circumstances of their lives. The episodes of suffering in "Eveline" and "After the Race" accentuate the inability of the protagonists to control the progression of events.

But in "Two Gallants," added later, the exposure of Lenehan's character gives a caustic effect in that we see how the protagonist's lack of will power and distorted sense of values make him suffer needlessly and endure a suffering whose causes he is unable to remedy.

"The Boarding House" exemplifies an episode of choice in which the constant element emphasized in the handling of the episode is some prominent attribute of the protagonist's moral character—in this case, Mrs. Mooney's expert prudential management of her affairs. As in "A Mother" and in "Counterparts," the habitual choices of Mrs. Kearney and Farrington demonstrated in the incidents arise from a part of their character which they cannot modify or transcend. The effect of this episode in "A Mother" is qualified sympathy for the distressed protagonist; in "Counterparts," a qualified horror. In contrast, the effect of the episode in "The Boarding House" is pleasurable, since the final emphasis is not on Mrs. Mooney's crafty and maybe vindictive foresight but on Doran's folly and on Polly's helpless, pathetic plight.

The remaining stories, dealing with maturity and public life, divide themselves into stories with painful and nonpainful effects. The nonpainful stories like "Clay," "Ivy Day in the Committee Room," "A Mother," and "Grace," stress, not the suffering of the protagonists, but their pursuit of certain objectives (or their determination to remain as they are without change), which reveals their vanity or some deficiency in moral or intellectual faculty. In "Grace" and "A Mother," we have episodes in which a habitual choice is reiterated through changing circumstances. In "Clay," the caustic effect of the reader's thwarted punitive desire is mingled with the pathos of Maria's helplessness. Pathos makes the character sufficiently interesting for us to enjoy our sense of superiority over her. In "Ivy Day in the Committee Room," all the characters except Crofton display an absurd defect which goes uncorrected and unpunished. Since no one is overtly aware of the harmful effect of the protagonists' behavior, pity and fear are precluded. The comic quality of this story, like that of "Grace," arises from the satisfaction we get from passing judgment on the absurdity of the action and from a feeling that some underlying justice is ratified in the end.

Pity and dread characterize the emotional effect of the painful stories: "A Little Cloud," "Counterparts," "A Painful Case," and "The Dead." Unlike the nonpainful stories, where we obtain pleasure directly from the contemplation of the ridiculous, the harmless ugliness of the characters, the painful stories give a pleasure derived from the catharsis of pain, a pleasure originating from the experience of a painful emotion that undergoes a complete development, as in "A Painful Case" and "The Dead." We witness an immediate development of the reversal that engenders the suffering, and this suffering is in turn purged by our perception of the inevitability of the protagonist's misfortune. In "A Little Cloud," the change in Little Chandler has a caustic element that neutralizes the fearful aspects of his disillusionment. Farrington's misfortune in "Counterparts" seems undeserved, yet our sympathy is alienated by his compulsive brutality in the end— a predictable but nonetheless horrifying act.

The composite emotional intentions of "The Dead" can be clarified by articulating our sympathy for the admirable qualities of Gabriel that overshadow his defects, so that in the vivid change of thought which possesses him we suffer with him. But the painful possibilities are thwarted short of full development by the protagonist's capacity to divest himself of his egotism, by his "negative capability," and this deprives the newly gained recognition of his own absurd defects from inflicting any harm on himself or on others. A genuine sense of purgation is accomplished in the loss of individual consciousness after

Gabriel's projection of himself in his antagonist's image, that of Michael Furey, and thus bringing about a reconciliation in the end of "The Dead."

Joyce's narrative craft in *Dubliners* has impressed readers and critics for its power to reveal the truth of character or circumstance with realistic economy and symbolic plenitude. What has not been clearly understood is how this craft is, in a sense, limited to a typical concentration on producing a kind of story whose power resides in the handling of a single episode. We have to go to *Ulysses* and *Finnegans Wake* for a real plot in the authentic epic sense.

All the stories, except "The Dead," depict a change of mood without the occurrence of any irreversible change of any importance. Nothing conclusive happens; what affects us often is the demonstration of what the characters have failed to learn—the need for discriminating between the romantic dreams that they mistake for reality and the actual demands of everyday life. The episodes that Joyce contrives serve as concrete manifestations of certain unchanged facts about the characters' relationship with himself and with others. We witness not an initial or final defeat, but a characteristic one. The stories in *Dubliners* may rightly be viewed as revelations of a static situation through episodes which are materializations of that situation. In "The Dead," however, Joyce represents an action containing an irreversible change, producing a complex pathos that magnificently redeems the artist from any charge of merciless truthfulness or compassionate lying.

In summary, we can say that in *Dubliners* Joyce composed two types of story: the episode of character or choice, and the episode of discovery, both of which have become the prevailing types of the modern short story from the nineteen-twenties on.

In the episode of character, the narrative action concentrates on the habitual choice that compels the protagonist to respond to varying situations without any radical alteration in his character. What the story presents are developing situations that provide the occasion for the protagonist to reiterate a habitual choice, thus evoking moral judgment in the reader. The clearest examples are "Eveline," "After the Race," "The Boarding House," "Clay," and "A Mother." In these stories, an important constant factor reasserts itself in the testing situations or ordeals; the change effected by the episode is secondary to the reiteration of a choice, since the character learns nothing and his motives remain unaltered. Other stories that exhibit this pattern are "Counterparts," "A Little Cloud," "Two Gallants," "Ivy Day in the Committee Room" and "Grace."

In the episode of discovery, the unifying action consists of a reversal of the protagonist's intentions and a discovery of his mistake or absurd defect, followed by an inner disturbance or suffering. Here the change that figures in the crisis of the protagonist's sensibility is largely a change of thought. In stories like "The Sisters," "An Encounter," "Araby," "A Painful Case" and "The Dead," the episode of discovery emphasizes the material of thought and feelings rather than the character or *ethos* it forms. The episode is unified by the change occurring in the thought of the protagonist (in the protagonists of the first three stories with an initiation theme) in Mr. Duffy of "A Painful Case" and Gabriel Conroy of "The Dead." It is true that Lenehan in "Two Gallants" and Farrington in "Counterparts" both experience a moment of awareness, but this awareness fails to assert itself effectively and is obscured by the characteristic patterns of thought and sentiment that sustain the protagonist's reiterated choice. Furthermore, the episode of discovery exhibits a unity not in progressive activity of any kind but in the narrator's devices of revelation.

A large part of the pleasure we experience in reading *Dubliners* comes from the degree of intellectual effort we expend in pursuing inferences that lead to the formulation of judgment and estimates of moral qualities residing in the action of the story. It is common knowledge that man delights in discovering and learning something, especially if in this process his mind apprehends beauty and truth in the integrity, consonance, and radiance of the artistic work.

One constant and immediate effect may be said to characterize our reading experience: an enlarged sense of being more self-critical and at the same time compassionate. This arises from the unique strategy of persuasion Joyce refers to as "scrupulous meanness," mentioned previously in the introduction. Joyce's style of "scrupulous meanness" is difficult to define because it is not just a product of linguistic habit or symbolic ingenuity but rather a total impression evoked by techniques of representation, characterization, and arrangement of incidents—in short, everything that enters into the shaping of the narrative action. "Scrupulous" would refer to the degree of objectivity and clarity in the analysis of experience. This analysis entails distance and perspective, sensitive observation, an attitude of integral thoroughness sufficient to establish a large framework governing the selection of all the details and their purposive disposition. "Meanness" would signify not so much a certain malicious or cruel strain in the presentation of truth as a certain equilibrium of sensibility (Joyce would not withhold a pun here), a mean between sentimental empathy and impersonal criticism, a balance between feelingful involvement and rational consciousness. Equilibrium requires a sure and accurate grasp of the complex forces interacting in experience—that is, "scrupulousness" in the selection and arrangement of details within a harmonious ordering of the whole.

Joyce once defined the ideal aesthetic attitude as one of stasis, an equilibrium of contradictory forces. It involves a mind arrested, freed from desire (pity) and loathing (terror). The arrest of the mind "is necessary for the ap-

prehension of the beautiful—the end of all art, tragic or
comic—for this rest is the only condition under which the
images, which are to excite in us terror or pity or joy, can
be properly presented to us and properly seen by us. For
beauty is a quality of something seen but terror and pity
and joy are states of the mind."[5] Pity and terror are arrested when the artist modulates the distance between us
and his characters by counterpointing the characters' attractive qualities with the limiting circumstances they find
themselves in, judging character as agents responsible for
their choices and actions.

Conjoined with the idea of stasis, "scrupulous meanness" would signify justice and reality bound together in
a single composite work, an imitation of action that is
unified and complete, giving a pleasure proper to its form.

The achievement of *Dubliners* may aptly be expressed
as a transubstantiation of life's sensory flux into form.
Joyce called his stories "a series of epicleti"—*epiklesis*
refers to an invocation of the Holy Ghost to transform the
consecrated wafer and wine into the body and blood of
Christ.[6] Joyce thus compares the imaginative process to the
Eucharist. Affirming the hieratic power of the artist to
transubstantiate the particulars of experience into a universal form, Joyce further clarifies his method: "There is
a certain resemblance between the mystery of the Mass
and what I am trying to do . . . to give people a kind of
intellectual pleasure or spiritual enjoyment by converting
the bread of everyday life into something that has a permanent artistic life of its own . . . for their mental, moral,
and spiritual uplift."[7] What finally appears significant

5. Entry dated 13 February 1903 in Joyce's Paris Notebook, reproduced
in *The Workshop of Daedalus*, ed. Robert Scholes and Richard M. Kain
(Evanston, Ill.: Northwestern University Press, 1965), pp. 53–54.
6. Robert Scholes and A. Walton Litz, eds., *Dubliners* (New York:
Viking Press, 1969), p. 255. See Joyce's letter to Constantine Curran,
August 1904.
7. *Letters of James Joyce*, edited by Richard Ellman (New York: Viking
Press, 1966), vol. 2, p. 169.

after elucidating the form of fiction and the narrative craft illustrated by *Dubliners* is the fact that the unremitting creative impulse behind the book originates from the need of the artist to deliver his criticism of life in complex unified actions, ambiguous in their philosophical implications but exact in their ultimate effects. If the stories lack "finality," as some readers allege, it is because they focus on episodes involving gradual intensification and disclosure of situations whose moral and affective meaning can be determined only after engaging in a long, intricate process of inference. Given the choice of subject and the type of form elected by the artist, *Dubliners* succeeds in transmitting an image of men in action endowed with the quality of felt understanding—the classic hallmark of its enduring life.

BIBLIOGRAPHICAL NOTE
AND
SELECTED BIBLIOGRAPHY

The edition of *Dubliners* used in this book is the definitive one edited by Robert Scholes and A. Walton Litz for the Viking Critical Library, copyright 1969 by The Viking Press, Inc. It includes the more significant critical articles and notes on the stories and a selected bibliography. The present study was completed long before the appearance of *James Joyce's Dubliners: Critical Essays,* edited by Clive Hart (London: Faber and Faber, 1969). A useful collection of criticism is *Twentieth Century Interpretations of Dubliners: A Collection of Critical Essays,* edited by Peter K. Garrett (Englewood Cliffs, N.J.: Prentice Hall, Inc., 1968).

For a complete catalogue of critical and interpretive studies of *Dubliners,* the student should consult the *PMLA* annual listing and the following bibliographies: Robert H. Deming, *A Bibliography of James Joyce Studies* (Lawrence, Kan.: University of Kansas Libraries, 1964), and the recent exhaustive bibliography in the James Joyce Special Number of *Modern Fiction Studies* 15 (Spring 1969): 105–82.

Selected Bibliography
(Books and articles referred to in the work)

Adams, Robert M. *James Joyce: Common Sense and Beyond.* New York: Random House, 1966.

Benstock, Bernard. "Arabesques: Third Position of Concord." *James Joyce Quarterly* 5 (Fall 1967) : 30–39.

———. " 'The Sisters' and the Critics." *James Joyce Quarterly* 4 (Fall 1966) : 32–35.

Brodbar, Harold. "A Religious Allegory: Joyce's 'A Little Cloud.' " *Midwest Quarterly* (Spring 1961), pp. 221–29.

Burke, Kenneth. *Perspective by Incongruity.* Edited by Stanley Edgar Hyman. Bloomington, Ind.: Indiana University Press, 1964.

Connolly, Thomas. "Joyce's 'The Sisters': A Pennyworth of Snuff." *College English* 27 (1965) : 189–95.

Crane, R. S. "The Concept of Plot and the Plot of *Tom Jones.*" *Critics and Criticism Ancient and Modern,* edited by R. S. Crane. Chicago and London: University of Chicago Press, 1952.

Ellmann, Richard. *James Joyce.* New York: Oxford University Press, 1959.

Friedrich, Gerhard. "The Perspective of Joyce's *Dubliners.*" *College English* 26 (1965) : 421–26.

Garrett, Peter K., ed. *Twentieth-Century Interpretations of Dubliners.* Englewood Cliffs, N.J.: Prentice-Hall, 1968.

Ghiselin, Brewster. "The Unity of Joyce's *Dubliners.*" *Accent* 16 (Spring 1956) : 75–88; (Summer 1956) : 196–213.

Gifford, Don. *Notes for Joyce.* New York: Dutton, 1967.

Goldman, Arnold. *The Joyce Paradox: Form and Free-*

dom in His Fiction. Evanston, Ill.: Northwestern University Press, 1966.

Joyce, James. *Critical Writings of James Joyce*. Edited by Richard Ellmann and Ellsworth Mason. New York: Viking Press, 1959.

———. *Dubliners*. Edited by Robert Scholes in consultation with Richard Ellmann. New York: Viking Press, 1967.

———. *The Letters of James Joyce*. vol. 1, edited by Stuart Gilbert. New York: Viking Press, 1957. vols. 2 and 3 edited by Richard Ellman. New York: Viking Press, 1966.

———. *A Portrait of the Artist as a Young Man:* The Definitive Text, corrected from the Dublin Holograph by Chester G. Anderson and edited by Richard Ellmann. New York: Viking Press, 1964.

———. *Stephen Hero*. Edited by Theodore Spencer. New York: New Directions, new ed., 1963.

———. *The Workshop of Daedalus: James Joyce and the Materials for* A Portrait of the Artist as a Young Man. Edited by Robert Scholes and Richard M. Kain. Evanston, Ill.: Northwestern University Press, 1965.

Joyce, Stanislaus. "The Background to *Dubliners.*" *The Listener* 51 (March 25, 1954) : 526–27.

Kenner, Hugh. *Dublin's Joyce*. Boston: Beacon Press reissue, 1962.

Levin, Harry. *James Joyce*. Norfolk, Conn.: New Directions, 1941.

Magalaner, Marvin. "Joyce, Nietzsche, and Hauptmann in James Joyce's 'A Painful Case.'" *PMLA* 68 (1953) : 95–102.

——— and Richard M. Kain. *Joyce The Man The Work The Reputation*. New York: New York University Press, 1956.

————. *Time of Apprenticeship: The Fiction of Young James Joyce.* New York: Abelard-Schuman, 1959.

Noon, William. "Joyce's 'Clay': An Interpretation." *College English* 17 (November 1955): 93–95.

Olson, Elder, ed. *Aristotle's Poetics and English Literature.* Chicago: University of Chicago Press, 1965.

————. *Tragedy and the Theory of Drama.* Detroit, Michigan: Wayne State University Press, 1966 reprint.

Ruoff, James. " 'A Little Cloud': Joyce's Portrait of the Would-Be Artist." *Research Studies of the State College of Washington* 25 (September 1957): 256–71.

Staley, Thomas F. "Moral Responsibility in Joyce's 'Clay.' " *Renascence* 18 (1966): 125–28.

Stein, William Bysshe. "The Effects of Eden in Joyce's 'Eveline.' " *Renascence* 15 (Spring 1963): 124–26.

Stone, Harry. " 'Araby' and the Writings of James Joyce." *Antioch Review* 25 (Fall 1965): 375–410.

Telford, Kenneth. *Aristotle's Poetics: Translation and Analysis.* Chicago, Ill.: Regnery, 1961.

Tindall, William York. *A Reader's Guide to James Joyce.* New York: Noonday Press, 1959.

Walzl, Florence. "Pattern of Paralysis in Joyce's *Dubliners.*" *College English* 22 (1961): 221–28.

Wright, Austin McGiffert. *The American Short Story in the Twenties.* Chicago: University of Chicago Press, 1961.

INDEX

action, 10, 19, 21, 23–27, 34, 45, 51, 56, 80, 88–89, 95, 98, 101, 117, 120, 126, 133, 148, 152, 156–58, 161, 164–65, 169, 170–71, 180–82, 194, 206, 212, 215–17, 225, 232–40, 244–48. *See also* Imitation; Plot; Sequence
admiration, 135, 200
aesthetic object, 26
aesthetic theory, 27
aesthetics, 20
agent, 23. *See also* Character
alienation, 19, 27, 43, 64, 122, 128, 141, 163, 179, 186. *See also* Estrangement
allegory, 15–16, 117, 147, 176, 215, 235. *See also* Emblem
allusions, 96, 99, 146, 216, 225
ambiguity, 10, 44, 60, 81, 113, 148, 173, 204, 236, 248
ambivalence, 45–46, 76, 81, 90, 100
anagnorisis, 236. *See also* Discovery; Recognition
anagram, 76
analogy, 24, 80, 86, 122, 162, 169, 105–6, 213, 225, 233–34. *See also* Correspondence; Parallelism
analogical matrix, 62
analysis, 21–22, 169, 211–12, 214, 234, 238, 246
anecdote, 199, 235

animism, 60
anti-hero, 123, 191
antithesis, 94, 113, 126, 143, 180, 183
appropriateness, 128, 206. *See also* Decorum; Propriety
archetypal myth, 15, 147, 235. *See also* Myth
argument, 17, 24, 27, 39, 80, 106, 119, 166, 235
Aristotle, 24, 67
artist, 66, 247
asceticism, 163
association (verbal), 123, 164, 215
assonance, 35
atmosphere, 74, 84, 107, 130, 144, 152, 170, 179, 219
attitude, 134, 163, 181–83, 189, 217, 225
authority, 45, 49, 65, 103, 120–21, 142; narrative, 148, 184, 194, 238

Bacchus, 179
bathos, 181
beauty, perception of, 21–22, 25, 246–47
behavior, 91; logic of, 95, 113, 117, 128, 179, 183, 190, 230
bourgeois marriage, 94; urban, 144
Burke, Kenneth, 211–13
burlesque, 86, 97, 227. *See also* Parody; Satire